Ginger Salad and Water Wafers

Recipes from Myanmar

By Ma Thanegi

Photographs by Tiffany Wan

Ginger Salad and Water Wafers
Recipes from Myanmar
by Ma Thanegi
Photographs by Tiffany Wan

Copy-editing by Sheri Quirt
Cover and book design by Tiffany Wan

ThingsAsian Press, San Francisco, California. USA

www.thingsasianpress.com
Printed in Hong Kong
ISBN-10: 1-934159-25-5
ISBN-13: 978-1-934159-25-5

This book is dedicated with love to my mother,
Daw May Tin Tut,
who all her life loved good food but refused to cook,
apart from four great dishes she made to perfection.

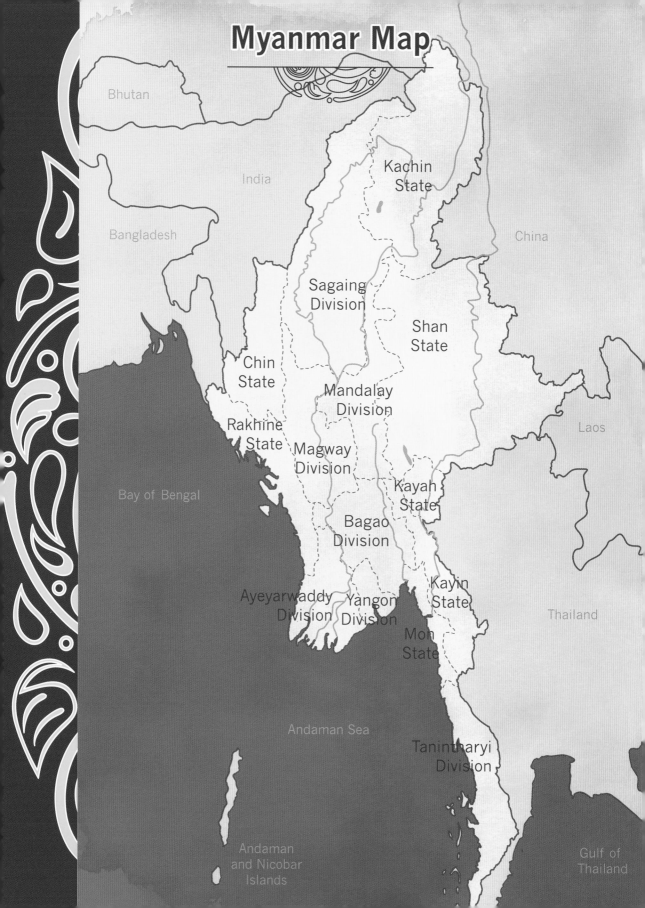

Myanmar Map

Bhutan

India

Bangladesh

China

Kachin State

Sagaing Division

Shan State

Chin State

Mandalay Division

Rakhine State

Magway Division

Bay of Bengal

Laos

Kayah State

Bagao Division

Kayin State

Ayeyarwaddy Division

Yangon Division

Thailand

Mon State

Andaman Sea

Tanintharyi Division

Andaman and Nicobar Islands

Gulf of Thailand

Contents

Noodles   115

Desserts   139

Snacks   153

Appreciation

As I am a keen cook and at present too busy with other things to do so on a regular basis, one of my chief pleasures is to talk food in all its aspects with friends who are famous for their culinary skills. During such conversations over the years I have picked many a great cook's brain.

To name but a few they are:
Daw Kitty Than Naing, who should be writing a cookbook of her own,
Daw Maibelle Tun Mra, who taught me the finer points,
Daw Khin Khin Morvan, who generously told me all her shortcut secrets,
Wendy San San Thynn, who helped with the test-cooking and tasting,
Ruby Khin Myint Khine, excellent kitchen manager with great tips and recipes,
Dahlia Khin Nyunt Yee, expert on sweets,
Sandra Khyn Ma Ma, my consultant on menus and traditional dishes,
Tammy Mya Mya Win, who makes the best monhinga,
Nang Kham Ohng, who cooks great Shan food,
Ruby Kyaw Maung, always ready to share her techniques,
Thi Thi Ta, a wonderful hostess who must write her own cookbook,
Nyo Ye Myint Pe, an excellent source for many recipes, and
Amy Nyein, a perfect hand with salads.

All of them love to cook for others and talk food, and they throw fabulous parties.

Having failed to persuade, beg, and threaten some of the above to write their own cookbooks, I finally had to do it myself. Their recipes, tips, and menus and those of others too numerous to mention by name have been incorporated into this book.

My thanks also to Gill Pattison and Juliana Tan for checking over the text, and Rosebud Mu Mu for checking the recipes. Thank you very much, all of you, aar lone kyay zu a myaar gyi tin bar dai...

Introduction

In Myanmar, to be Ei Wuk Kyay, which means to be hospitable, is the criterion of perfect social behavior. Our food culture is based on sharing: with monks to whom many of the Buddhist Myanmar offer food on a daily basis or on special occasions called Soon Kyway, and sharing lunchboxes among school friends or colleagues at work. Food and drink are offered free on special religious days in a ritual known as S'du Di Thar. Travelers stopping by a village would be welcomed to share a meal at the monastery, if not at someone's house. It gives not only joy but great merit to feed others with a generous heart, and this Buddhist concept rules the social life of the people.

In the past, there were few restaurants where people could entertain, so it was up to the housewife to cook everything at home for invited guests. When guests are expected, even if they are close friends, the dishes must be varied enough to cover the entire dining table. Desserts, normally not eaten after meals, must be as many as the cook can manage to bake or steam. When friends drop in unexpectedly they are eagerly invited to join the family in a potluck meal, but to be sure the wife will hurry to the kitchen to whip up an omelet or a stir-fry.

The social life of the Myanmar Buddhists centers around the Soon Kyway ceremonies mentioned above, which often commemorate weddings, novitiation of sons, ear-borings of daughters, birthdays, or rituals in the name of deceased family members. Then breakfast or lunch is served to the monks. The guests, often numbering in the hundreds, are usually served easier-to-prepare fare such as noodles. If not being catered, such festivities are occasions for the neighborhood cooks to show off their skills, as everyone helps out at these affairs.

With 135 officially recorded ethnic races living in the country, I have chosen for this book the dishes normally eaten by the majority race Bama (Burmese), with a few Indian- or Chinese-style dishes so commonly enjoyed that they are considered part of our heritage. This does not mean that the cuisines of the other ethnic nationalities are not to be recorded: on the contrary, they have so many excellent dishes that these should be presented in a separate collection. However, I have included a few of the dishes so popular that to omit them would be a sin.

A Myanmar proverb says: "You most remember your loved ones when you are eating something good." I hope the sharing of our recipes, if not the actual dishes, will generate the same feelings of warmth and friendship, which are the inborn traits of the Myanmar people.

Useful Information

Myanmar meals are based on several dishes eaten together with rice. Thus the soup, curries, salads, cooked vegetables, relish, and accompanying raw or blanched vegetables are served and eaten at once. The most important aspect of the meal is the harmony of dishes served together to balance the basic flavors of sweet, sour, savory, creamy, bitter, astringent, salty, and hot, as well as to create interesting differences in the textures of chewy, smooth, crunchy, crisp, tender, and "bitey." Each mouthful of rice is as unique as one wants to make it, with different combinations of tastes and textures.

RECIPES

The recipes here have not been altered to suit Western taste but are presented in the form in which the modern Myanmar woman cooks the traditional dishes, with ingredients, techniques, and appliances that save time and effort.

Each recipe is for four large servings. Typical menus are given in the chapter for main dishes, with suggestions for accompanying dishes. There are no set rules, however, so try your own menus, balancing the taste and texture of each dish.

SEASONINGS

The amount of seasonings can be adjusted to one's taste, especially salt, paprika, lime juice, and green chillies.

WEIGHTS

Weights are given in pounds and ounces. One pound is approximately 500 grams, or 30 ticals in the Myanmar measure.

COOKING TIMES

Cooking times given are to be used as a guide only, as they can differ according to various conditions.

Basic Gravy Methods
HSI THUT, LONE CHET
To sauté the basic gravy mix of onion, garlic, and ginger before adding meat is the Hsi Thut method, which is better for the aroma of the dish than to simply combine the uncooked basic gravy ingredients with the meat and water before cooking, called the Lone Chet way. A slightly better Lone Chet method is to use fried onions instead of raw, combined with freshly pounded garlic and ginger. The smaller onions or shallots are better for the gravy base or for frying than the large juicy ones, which are best for salads.

Basic Gravy Mix, a shortcut
A HNIT
For a curry to serve four, chop 2 ounces of small peeled onions in the grinder. Then grind 4 peeled cloves of garlic and 3 thin slices ginger. Peel and remove seeds from 2 ripe tomatoes and whiz in the blender. Sauté the ground onion with ¼ teaspoon turmeric powder in ¼ cup oil for 3 minutes until golden. Stir often. Add the ground garlic and ginger and cook ½ minute more. Add ½ teaspoon sweet paprika to the cooking onion-garlic-ginger mix, and in a few seconds stir in the tomato paste and cook until oil sizzles and rises to the surface. This gravy serves as a base for most dishes. A larger batch made with five or more times the amounts given will keep for weeks in the freezer.

Catfish
NGA KHU OR NGA GYI
Myanmar cooks prefer the freshwater catfish that are about 10 inches in length. Bigger ones from the sea have tougher flesh and a stronger smell. Wash off the slimy coating on catfish or other scaleless fish by rubbing with tamarind paste or vinegar. Nga Gyi is smaller and flatter and considered tastier.

Chayote
GAW RA KHA THEE
A fruit shaped like a pear with a rugged surface and very thin skin, eaten as a vegetable. Wash well after peeling.

Chickpea powder, raw
PEI HMONT SEIN
Also called channa dhal or split pea flour. Chickpea powder is readily available in Indian groceries. Deep-fried whole chickpeas are also available.

Chickpea powder, roasted
PEI HMONT A KYET
Pan-fry chickpea powder on very low heat until it becomes fragrant and begins to turn slightly darker. Take care not to burn. Cool and store in an airtight jar.

Chilli powder, roasted dried red
NGA YOKE THEE HMONT
Pan-fry dried red chillies quickly on low heat, remove stems, and seeds too if preferred, and pound roughly. Store in an airtight jar.

Chinese pork sausage
WET OO CHAUNG
To fry, slice thinly and place in a wok with a little water and 1 teaspoon oil. Bring to a boil and keep on stirring until all the water has evaporated. Continue frying until crisp.

Clarified butter or Ghee
GHEE HTAW BUT
Sold in Indian food stores, ghee is used in Indian-style sweets, curries, and rice. Can be substituted with butter.

Coconut cream
OHN NO
Unsweetened coconut cream is available in cans or in powdered form from Asian groceries. Stir well before using. Solidifies very quickly when chilled.

Coriander
NAN NAN PIN
Chinese coriander
T'YOKE NAN NAN
Also called cilantro or Asian parsley. Chinese coriander looks similar but has bigger leaves and smells different.

Dried shrimp
PAZUN CHAUK
Grind in a clean coffee grinder until fluffy. If they are too big, cut into smaller pieces before grinding. The best ones are plump and red.

Drumstick fruit
DANT DA LUN THEE
Long, thin, and knobbly with a thick, fibrous peel, drumstick fruits are great in soups or in watery fish curries. The small and round leaves used in soups are medicinal: good for high blood pressure, as is Chinese coriander.

Dried red chillies
NGA YOKE THEE CHAUK
For traditional curry base, dried red chillies are first soaked in water to soften after removing stems and seeds, and then pounded to a paste. The easier way is to use sweet or hot paprika, according to preference.

Fermented fish, aka pickled fish
NGA PI YAY CHO
Available in cans or glass jars from Thai food stores.

Fish sauce
NGAN PYAR YAY
A thin, clear, dark red sauce made from shrimp, which gives the necessary authentic flavor to Asian cooking. It does not have a strong smell so it can be added straight from the bottle to cooked dishes.

Fried garlic and garlic oil
KYET THUN HPYU KYAW
KYET THUN HPYU HSI CHET
Crush, peel, and chop 3 1/2 ounces garlic. Heat 1 cup oil on medium heat and fry the garlic until golden and crisp, about 5 minutes. Remove pan from heat and immediately drain the garlic on absorbent paper. Take care not to burn. Store the cooled oil and fried garlic separately in airtight jars. This yields 1 cup fried garlic and 2/3 cup garlic oil.

Fried onion slices and onion oil
KYET THUN NI KYAW
KYET THUN NI HSI CHET
Peel and cut into uniform slices 3 ½ ounces of small onions. Put the onion slices with 1 cup oil in a pan on medium heat and fry until golden brown and crisp, about 5 minutes. Remove pan from heat and immediately drain the onion slices on absorbent paper. Store the cooled oil and fried onions separately in airtight jars. This yields 1 cup fried onions and 2/3 cup onion oil.

Galanga
BA DAI GAW
A fragrant and peppery root very much like ginger, used mostly in Rakhine cooking. The Rakhine race live on the west coast of Myanmar.

Garam masala
MASALA HMONT
Indian spice mix, readily available in Indian groceries. Myanmar do not grind these spices at home nor use a lot.

Garlic
KYET THUN HPYU
If not cutting into neat rounds, it is easier to peel garlic by first crushing it and cutting off the root part.

Gourd
BU THEE
Also called calabash or bottle-neck gourd, it has a light green, fuzzy skin and white flesh. Seeds if tender can be eaten.

Green chillies
NGA YOKE THEE SEIN
The mild, puffy ones are most fragrant and are the best for general use. The tiny ones are too hot.

Jaggery or palm sugar
HTA NYET
Produced from toddy palm juice in brown pellets of various hues and sizes. The darkest ones have the richest flavor. To make about ½ cup of syrup, boil 3 1/2 ounces jaggery pellets in 1/3 cup water for 5 minutes or until thick.

Lemongrass
ZA BA LIN
The heads are covered with tough layers, which should be peeled away if the lemongrass is to be pounded to add to gravy. If they are to be discarded after cooking, there is no need to strip off the outer layers.

Oil
HSI
We prefer peanut oil, but corn oil is a good substitute.

Onion
KYET THUN NI
The onions used in Myanmar are small, what in the West would be called shallots. If not cutting into rings, it is easier to peel onions by first cutting lengthwise, trimming off both ends, and lastly removing the skin.

Pickled bamboo shoots
MYIT CHIN
Sour pickled bamboo shoots are available in cans from Thai food stores.

Pickled tofu, aka fermented tofu
HSI TOFU
Widely available in Chinese markets, it is pungent and flavorful, rightly called the Cheese of the East.

Roasted rice powder
HSAN HLAW HMONT
Pan-roast raw rice until light brown, taking care not to burn, and grind roughly. Store in an airtight jar.

Roselle or Sorrel leaf
CHIN BAUNG YWET
Sour with a hint of bitterness, the leaves look like maple leaves. Sometimes available in Indian groceries.

Salted duck eggs
BAI U HSAR SEIN
Boil 2 tablespoons of salt in ½ cup water for each egg. Put eggs in a glass jar and pour in the cooled and sieved brine to cover. The eggs are ready in 2 weeks and eaten hard-boiled.

Semolina
SHWE JI
Also called Cream of Wheat, medium-rough semolina is best for making cakes. It should look like fine bran.

Shrimp paste
NGA PI SEIN SAR
Also called balachan, it is made from salted shrimp pounded to a smooth paste. The best shrimp paste is purplish-pink in color. It is easily cooked just by grilling lightly and can even be eaten raw.

Soda bicarbonate, aka Baking soda
SAAR HSAWDA
Adding 1/8 teaspoon to stock or boiling water helps green vegetables and leaves retain their color.

Soy sauce
PEI NGAN PYAR YAY
Both the light and the thick, dark versions must not be salty. We prefer the sweeter version.

Tamarind paste
MA JII HNIT
Tamarind is a knobbly, finger-length fruit with sour, brown flesh. It adds a piquant touch to curries and soups and makes a great fruit drink mixed with jaggery syrup.

Turmeric powder
HSA NWIN
A deep yellow powder ground from a root. Not only does it give a nice color to gravy, but it also removes the smell from meat and fish. It is used with salt to marinate the meat some minutes before cooking. Do not add to a dish already cooking or after it is cooked, as its raw smell is a bit unpleasant.

Main Dishes

Some curries are called Hsi Pyan Hin, which literally means a dish where the oil has "returned." This refers to the cooking process in which the basic gravy ingredients of pounded onions, garlic, and ginger together with the meat have been cooked with water and, when the liquid evaporates, the oil sizzles and rises to the surface in triumphant return. The other type of curry is the Yay Cho Hin, which has a watery gravy and much less oil. Fish or prawns are often cooked in this manner.

Pazun Doke Hsi Pyan
GIANT RIVER PRAWN CURRY

In Myanmar the giant river prawns can easily weigh up to ½ pound each. Get whole unpeeled prawns, as the red-gold cream in the head known as prawn oil is essential to all prawn curries. Considered a great delicacy, sometimes the cream is painstakingly gathered from many heads, cooked down, and eaten dribbled on warm rice or on ripe bananas as a dessert. The black grainy sac in the head is always removed, as are the two bony "fangs" in the jaws as well as the black spinal vein. We tend to cook our prawns until hard and chewy.

SERVE with plain rice, pumpkin flower soup, Thee Sone Thanut lightly pickled vegetables, and Nga Pi Lainmar, the well-behaved pickled fish, with raw and blanched vegetables.

INGREDIENTS

4 giant prawns or 8 prawns
Salt
1/4 teaspoon turmeric powder
1 tablespoon fish sauce
1/4 cup oil
2 onions, peeled and pounded

4 cloves garlic, peeled and pounded
1/4 teaspoon sweet paprika
2 ripe tomatoes, peeled and blended to a
  paste
2 tablespoons chopped green onions

DIRECTIONS

1. Wash and shell the prawns and cut away the legs. Leave the head intact but remove the black sac and the two bony "fangs" from the head by pulling them out through the front of the head. Make sure none of the prawn oil is lost. Remove the black spinal vein by cutting a shallow line along the spine. Leave on the tail if preferred. Lightly rub with a little salt and the turmeric powder and set aside for 5 minutes.

2. Heat the oil and sauté the pounded onions until golden brown, for 5 minutes. Add the pounded garlic and fry 1 minute more until fragrant. Then add the sweet paprika and the tomato paste and cook, stirring, for 2 minutes. Add the prawns and fish sauce and cook a few minutes until the prawns begin to curl, turning gently once. Add salt to taste. When the oil almost sizzles, sprinkle with green onions and remove from heat.

Pazun Yay Cho
PRAWNS IN WATERY GRAVY

Prawns or fish are sometimes cooked in watery gravy with some tomatoes and green chillies. These dishes are very easy to prepare and something that the busy housewife can cook just before the meal.

SERVE with plain rice, water spinach Chin Yay sour soup, Kha Yan Thee Hnut stuffed eggplant, and Nga Pi Htaung grilled shrimp paste with raw and blanched vegetables.

INGREDIENTS

1 1/2 pounds shrimps, washed and peeled
2 teaspoons oil
1 teaspoon fish sauce
1 onion, peeled and chopped roughly
3 cloves garlic, peeled and pounded

1/4 teaspoon turmeric powder
Salt
3 green chillies, stems and seeds removed
2 tablespoons chopped coriander or basil

DIRECTIONS

Mix all the ingredients together apart from the green chillies and cook until the shrimps are almost curled up. Stir in the green chillies. Add salt to taste. Top with the coriander or basil.

Kyet Thar Pyoke Kyaw
DRY-ROASTED CHICKEN

This is an easy way to cook chicken and considered the best invalid food. It is delicious with just a plate of warm rice and a clear soup. Myanmar cooks turn up their noses at battery hens, and indeed the sweetness of a tender free-range drumstick has to be tasted to be believed

SERVE with plain rice, bamboo shoots and shrimp soup, Long Bean Salad, and Nga Pi Yay pickled fish relish with raw and blanched vegetables.

INGREDIENTS

1 3/4 pounds free-range chicken, cut into medium pieces
4 cloves garlic, peeled and crushed
1 thin slice ginger, chopped
1/8 teaspoon turmeric powder

1 teaspoon dark soy sauce
6 tablespoons oil
3 potatoes, peeled and halved
Salt
Pepper

DIRECTIONS

1. Combine all of the ingredients apart from the potatoes, kneading well into the chicken.

2. Add ½ cup water and cook on low heat until the chicken is almost tender, adding water as necessary. Add the potatoes and continue simmering until both the chicken pieces and the potatoes are tender.

Kyet Thar Hsi Pyan
CHICKEN CURRY

Any meal to be served to monks or guests must include the Very Honorable dish of chicken curry, so much so that just ten minutes after their arrival, any visitor to a villager's house can expect to hear the shrieks of hens as they are chased in the backyard.

SERVE with plain rice, tomato Chin Yay sour soup, Pyaungbu Htaung Kyaw creamy corn, Winged Bean Salad and Ngan Pyar Yay Hpyaw fish sauce relish with raw and blanched vegetables. With coconut rice, serve clear roselle soup, Daikon Salad, and Balachaung with raw cucumbers.

INGREDIENTS

1 3/4 pounds free-range chicken

1/4 teaspoon turmeric powder

Salt

1/4 cup oil

3 onions, peeled and pounded

4 cloves garlic, peeled and pounded

2 thin slices ginger, pounded

1/2 teaspoon sweet paprika

1 head of lemongrass, crushed

DIRECTIONS

1. Cut the chicken into medium pieces: 2 pieces from each breast, legs into thighs and drumsticks, and wings cut away but left whole. Knead well with salt and 1/8 teaspoon turmeric powder. Let stand 10 minutes.

2. Heat the oil with 1/8 teaspoon of turmeric powder and sauté the pounded onions until golden brown, for 5 minutes. Add the pounded garlic and ginger and fry 1 minute more until fragrant. Add the sweet paprika and almost immediately add the chicken and the lemongrass. Cook, stirring, to seal the surface of the chicken.

3. Add ½ cup water, reduce heat, cover the pot, and simmer until all the liquid has evaporated and you hear oil sizzling. Prod the chicken with a spoon to see if it's tender; if not, add a bit more water. Stir a few times so that the chicken does not stick to the pot. When the oil sizzles and separates from the gravy, remove pot from heat. Discard the lemongrass before serving.

Bai Thar Ban Darloo
DUCK VINDALOO

Vindaloo is a dish that originated in the Portuguese colony of Goa. Portuguese mercenaries had been serving in Southeast Asian armies around the 15th century, and their culinary legacy in Myanmar, as in many other lands, is "Vindaloo."

SERVE with Lentil and Butter Rice, clear roselle soup, Balachaung, and a salad of Thee Sone Thanut pickles.

INGREDIENTS

1 3/4 pounds duck, cut into medium pieces
3 tablespoons yogurt
1/8 teaspoon turmeric powder
Salt
5 cloves garlic, peeled and pounded
2 thin slices ginger, pounded
1/4 cup oil

3 crushed bay leaves
1 stick cinnamon
4 tablespoons fried onion slices ("Useful Information")
3 potatoes, peeled and cut into halves
1 teaspoon garam masala

DIRECTIONS

1. Cut the duck into medium pieces: 2 pieces from each breast, legs into thighs and drumsticks, and wings cut away but left whole. Prick with a fork all over and knead well with the salt, turmeric powder, and the yogurt. Let stand 3 hours in the refrigerator.

2. Heat the oil and sauté the bay leaves, cinnamon sticks, garlic, and ginger until fragrant, for 1 minute. Add the duck pieces and cook, stirring often, to seal the surface of the duck.

3. Add water to just cover, crumble in the fried onion slices, reduce heat, cover pot, and simmer until all the liquid has evaporated and oil sizzles. Stir a few times to prevent sticking. Check the tenderness of the duck and if still tough, add more water.

4. With the last addition of water, put in the potatoes. When the oil sizzles and separates from the gravy, sprinkle with 1 teaspoon garam masala, stir, and remove the pot from heat. Discard bay leaves and cinnamon before serving.

Bai La Hpet Thar Hsi Pyan
DUCK WITH PICKLED TEA LEAVES

This dish was cooked for me years ago by a wonderful couple. It combines the succulent fat of the duck with our famous pickled tea leaves. Usually we eat pickled tea leaves after a meal, but this combination was out of this world. Ordinary tea leaves or even fresh ones would not do. I'm afraid this essential ingredient is not easy to come by outside of Myanmar, unless you go to the few Myanmar shops in the main cities, search on the Internet, or ask a Myanmar friend to supply you with some.

SERVE with plain rice, a clear soup, Stir-fried Water Spinach, Grilled Eggplant Salad, and Nga Pi Yay pickled fish relish with raw and blanched vegetables.

INGREDIENTS

1 3/4 pounds duck, cut into medium pieces
1/8 teaspoon turmeric powder
Salt
1/4 cup oil
3 onions, peeled and pounded

4 cloves garlic, peeled and pounded
2 thin slices ginger, pounded
3 tablespoons ready-to-eat savory pickled tea leaves (not the sour or hot kind)

DIRECTIONS

1. Cut the duck into medium pieces: 2 pieces from each breast, legs into thighs and drumsticks, and wings cut away but left whole. Knead well with salt and 1/8 teaspoon turmeric powder. Let stand 10 minutes.

2. Heat the oil with 1/8 teaspoon turmeric powder and sauté the pounded onions until golden brown, for 5 minutes. Add the pounded garlic and ginger and fry 1 minute more until fragrant. Add the duck and cook, stirring often, to seal the surface of the duck.

3. Add water to cover and lower heat. Simmer until the duck is tender, adding more water as needed.

4. When just a little liquid remains, add the pickled tea leaves. Stir to prevent sticking. When oil separates from the gravy, remove pot from heat.

Kyet Thar Kar La Thar Chet
CURRY OF THE VILLAGE LADS

During the hot summer nights the young bachelors of each village stay up for "fire-alarm duty" and to drink toddy. Unmarried lads are called Kar La Thar, the Sons of the Times, and this recipe is for their supper. To prepare it, they must first raid someone's henhouse and another's gourd trellis for a dish that is understandably cooked in a hurry and consumed at a fast pace. It tastes as delicious when the ingredients are legally obtained.

SERVE with plain rice, Shaut Thee Thoke citrus salad, and Nga Pi Htaung grilled shrimp paste.

INGREDIENTS

1 young free-range chicken, cleaned and cut into small pieces

1/4 of a gourd, peeled and cut into cubes slightly bigger than the chicken

3 onions, peeled and chopped roughly

4 cloves garlic, peeled and crushed

2 thin slices ginger

2 heads lemongrass, crushed

1 teaspoon shrimp paste softened in a little water

1/4 teaspoon turmeric powder

1/2 teaspoon sweet paprika

A handful of coriander stalks, chopped roughly

1 tablespoon oil

Salt

DIRECTIONS

1. Mix all of the ingredients apart from the gourd and coriander in a pot, including all edible if bony parts of the chicken. Knead the chicken pieces thoroughly with the seasonings. Place the pot on fire and cook, stirring, until oil sizzles, then add water to cover.

2. When the chicken is tender, add the gourd and more water to make a soupy dish and let boil again until the gourd is tender. Remove the ginger slices and lemongrass, garnish with the coriander, and serve immediately.

Nga Myin Hsi Pyan
BUTTERFISH CURRY

Butterfish is the English name given to our Nga Myin or the less expensive Nga Dan, both huge freshwater scaleless fish with creamy, tender flesh. Nga Myin, highly prized, has a light yellow tinge to its flesh and is sweeter and creamier. Halibut or cod makes a good substitute.

SERVE with plain rice, Chicken Broth with Lime Leaves, Bamboo Shoots with Shrimps, and Pazun Hsait Nga Yoke Thee Hpyaw spicy shrimp relish with raw and blanched vegetables.

INGREDIENTS

1 1/2 pounds butterfish or cod filets, cut into 1 x 1 x 1-inch chunks
Salt
1/4 teaspoon turmeric powder
1/4 cup oil
3 onions, peeled and pounded

5 cloves garlic, peeled and pounded
3 thin slices ginger, pounded
1/3 teaspoon sweet paprika
2 ripe tomatoes, peeled and chopped
1 1/2 teaspoons fish sauce
1 tablespoon chopped coriander

DIRECTIONS

1. Knead the fish with salt to taste and the turmeric powder and let stand for 5 minutes.

2. Heat the oil and sauté the pounded onions until golden brown, about 5 minutes. Add the pounded garlic and ginger and fry 1/2 minute until fragrant. Add the sweet paprika and almost immediately add the tomatoes and the fish sauce. Cook for 2 minutes.

3. Put in the fish filets with 2 tablespoons of water and after 2 minutes turn them over gently.

4. Cook until the fish filets are done. When the oil separates from the gravy, garnish with the chopped coriander, and remove pot from heat.

Nga Tha Laut Paung
TENDER-TO-THE-BONE HILSA

One of our best fish dishes is the hilsa cooked until its many bones melt at a bite. Hilsa is often available frozen in Indian stores. Shad can be substituted. The large amount of 5% acidity vinegar is necessary to soften all the bones, but it is mild enough not to add a sour taste to the fish.

SERVE with plain rice, Red Lentil Soup, Stir-Fried Water Spinach, and Nga Pi Lainmar, the well-behaved pickled fish, with raw and blanched vegetables.

INGREDIENTS

1 3/4 pounds hilsa, scaled and cut into at least 4-inch-thick chunks
3/4 cup of 5% acidity vinegar
3 tablespoons light, sweet soy sauce
1/2 tablespoon ginger juice
1/4 teaspoon turmeric powder
1/2 teaspoon sugar
1/2 teaspoon salt

1/4 cup oil
3 onions, peeled and quartered
4 cloves garlic, peeled and pounded
1/2 teaspoon sweet paprika
1 ripe tomato, peeled and chopped
4 stalks lemongrass, preferably with leaves
6 whole peeled small shallots
2 tablespoons chopped green onions or coriander

DIRECTIONS

1. Knead the hilsa with all of the other ingredients apart from the shallots and green onions or coriander and let stand 10 minutes.

2. In a medium-sized pressure cooker, line the bottom with the lemongrass stalks, wedging them across the width of the pot so that they stay in place. Place the fish pieces on this plus the marinade. Steam for about 30 minutes with the maximum amount of water according to cooker instructions. When done, remove lid and continue cooking until oil sizzles.

3. If you do not have a pressure cooker, use any heavy, nonstick deep pot with the bottom lined with lemongrass as above. Simmer the hilsa on moderately low heat for about 5 hours with water to cover, adding more water as needed. Do not stir.

4. Test a bone to see if it is softened and when the bones begin to turn white and are soft, remove the lemongrass. Continue simmering until very little water remains, then add the whole peeled shallots and cook until they turn translucent.

5. When the oil separates from the gravy, remove the pot from heat and serve sprinkled with the coriander or green onions. Handle the fish carefully, but hilsa is firm-fleshed so it does not break easily even after long hours of cooking.

Nga But Hmwe
FLUFFY FISH

Nga But is a freshwater fish that has a strong smell, so we fry it with lots of lemongrass and ginger.

SERVE with plain rice, drumstick soup, Bitter Gourd with shrimp or pork, Nga Pi Yay pickled fish relish with raw and blanched vegetables.

INGREDIENTS

1 1/2 pounds Nga But
1/2 cup oil
1/4 teaspoon turmeric powder
1 onion, peeled and pounded
3 cloves garlic, peeled and pounded
4 slices ginger, pounded

2 heads lemongrass, sliced thinly and then pounded
1 teaspoon fish sauce
Salt
Fried onion slices ("Useful Information")

DIRECTIONS

1. Lightly poach the fish in a little water with salt to taste and 1/8 teaspoon turmeric powder. Cool and flake off flesh, discarding bones.

2. Heat the oil with 1/8 teaspoon turmeric powder and fry the pounded onion, garlic, ginger, and lemongrass for 2 minutes. Add the fish flakes with salt and fish sauce to taste and fry, stirring, until the fish is golden. Add salt to taste. Serve garnished with fried onions.

Nga Khu Sin Kaw
CHOPPED CATFISH

This is one of the best ways of cooking freshwater catfish. The leaves are from the noni plant (*Morinda angustifolia*), which is a medicinal herb, but mustard greens without the stalks can be substituted.

SERVE with plain rice, Thick Vegetable and Chickpea Soup, Stuffed Eggplant, and Mandalay Nga Pi Chet shrimp paste relish with raw and blanched vegetables.

INGREDIENTS

1 1/2 pounds freshwater catfish cut into strips, bones removed
Salt
Fish sauce to taste
1/8 teaspoon turmeric powder
1/4 cup oil

1 onion, peeled and sliced
4 cloves garlic, peeled and chopped
2 thin slices ginger, pounded
1 loosely packed cup of tender noni leaves or mustard leaves, thinly sliced

DIRECTIONS

1. Knead the fish with salt, fish sauce, and the turmeric powder and set aside for 5 minutes. Heat the oil and sauté the onion slices until fragrant for 1 minute, then add the chopped garlic and ginger and fry for ½ minute.

2. Add the fish with 1/4 cup water and cook until oil sizzles and begins to separate from the gravy. Stir in the sliced leaves and continue cooking until the leaves are wilted.

Ngar Kyaw Chet
FISH FRIED-STEWED

We eat freshwater fish a lot, as they are abundantly found in our clean streams and rivers. This is a simple and delicious way to cook fish with soft flesh, such as carp or snakehead.

SERVE with plain rice, clear soup, stewed beans, and Ngan Pyar Yay Hpyaw fish sauce relish with raw and blanched vegetables.

INGREDIENTS

1 1/2 pounds carp
Salt
1/8 teaspoon + 1/4 teaspoon turmeric powder
Oil for deep-frying
3 tablespoons oil

4 cloves garlic, peeled and pounded
2 ripe tomatoes, peeled and chopped roughly
1 large onion, cut into thick rings
1 tablespoon light soy sauce
Chopped green onions

DIRECTIONS

1. Cut the fish into 8 pieces and rub with salt and 1/8 teaspoon turmeric powder. Let stand 5 minutes and deep-fry until red-gold and crisp, about 10 minutes. Drain and set aside.

2. Heat 3 tablespoons oil with 1/4 teaspoon turmeric powder and sauté the pounded garlic for 1/2 minute. Add the chopped tomatoes and 3 tablespoons water.

3. Cook until the tomatoes are softened and add the fish, the onion rings, light soy sauce, and salt to taste. Simmer 2 minutes and sprinkle with the chopped green onions.

Ah-mei Hnut
CHUNKY BEEF STEW

This tender beef stew is traditionally cooked in large quantities on a charcoal fire so that the simmering juices and gravy work their magic on the meat. Cooking on low heat in a modern kitchen will do just as well.

SERVE with plain rice, tomato Chin Yay sour soup, Up-country Butter Beans, and Roasted Dried Chilli Relish with raw and blanched vegetables.

INGREDIENTS

1 1/2 pounds beef tenderloin, cut into 3/4 x 3/4 x 1-inch chunks (If using other cuts, you may need to use a tenderizer. One peeled and mashed kiwifruit or ¼ of a green papaya works well.)

1/8 teaspoon turmeric powder

1 teaspoon dark soy sauce

Salt

3 cloves garlic, peeled and pounded or ground

2 thin slices ginger, pounded

1/4 cup oil

4 tablespoons fried onion slices ("Useful Information")

6 whole peeled small shallots

DIRECTIONS

1. Prick the beef all over with a fork and knead well with salt, turmeric powder, dark soy sauce, and tenderizer if needed. Let stand 3 hours or overnight in the refrigerator. If using kiwifruit, do not marinate overnight. Alternatively, you can add a 3-inch chunk of green papaya to the cooking process.

2. In 1/4 cup oil, sauté the pounded garlic and ginger for ½ minute until fragrant.

3. Add the beef and cook, stirring, to seal the surface of the meat. Add water to cover, salt to taste, and crumble in the fried onion slices. Reduce heat and simmer until the beef is nearly tender, adding more water as necessary. Stir a few times as the meat cooks.

4. Add the whole peeled shallots when just a little liquid remains and remove pot from heat when the oil separates from the gravy.

Nga Hsoke Yay Cho
FISH CAKES IN WATERY GRAVY

Fish paste cakes are versatile: they can be made into a salad, garnish noodle dishes, eaten deep-fried as hors d'oeuvres, and added to soups. We use featherback fish with its flesh scraped off and pounded, but if unavailable, use carp or other white-fleshed fish or even the ready-made fish paste. The harder the fish paste is pounded the chewier it is, and I find it easier to use a grinder than a stone mortar.

SERVE with plain rice, Thick Sweet Gourd Soup, Grilled Eggplant Salad, and Pan Htway Hpyaw grilled tomato relish with raw and blanched vegetables.

INGREDIENTS

2 cups fish paste
1 onion, peeled and chopped
3 cloves garlic, peeled and chopped
2 thin slices ginger, pounded
Salt
Oil for frying
2 tablespoons oil
1/8 teaspoon turmeric powder

1 onion, chopped finely
1/3 teaspoon sweet paprika
1 tablespoon tamarind paste softened in a
   little water
1 teaspoon fish sauce
1 tablespoon chopped coriander
3 green chillies, stems and seeds removed

DIRECTIONS

1. Grind the fish paste, salt, chopped onion, garlic, and ginger together. Wet your hands and form the fish paste into coin-sized rounds. Fry until golden, drain, and set aside.

2. Heat 2 tablespoons oil with the turmeric powder and sauté the finely chopped onions until fragrant, 1 minute. Add the sweet paprika and the fish cakes with the fish sauce and green chillies. Simmer until oil sizzles, add the tamarind paste with a little water, and let boil again once. Add salt to taste. Garnish with the coriander. The gravy should be watery.

Wet Thar Hin Lay
STEWED SOUR PORK

Pork has so much fat that to be able to eat lots of it, we balance it by adding sour ingredients. Traditionally this recipe uses Asian gooseberries, wild plums, and green tamarind, but roselle leaves or green mango work almost as well.

SERVE with plain rice, a clear soup, Spinach Salad, and Balachaung with raw and blanched vegetables.

INGREDIENTS

1 1/2 pounds pork rump, with skin
1 tablespoon fish sauce
1/2 teaspoon shrimp paste
3 tablespoons oil
Salt

1 onion, peeled and pounded
4 cloves garlic, peeled and pounded
2 cups loosely packed roselle leaves or 1 shredded green mango

DIRECTIONS

1. Cut the pork into medium chunks, prick all over, and knead well with salt and fish sauce. Set aside 5 minutes.

2. Mix the pork with all the other ingredients and knead well again. Place the pot on heat and cook, stirring, until oil sizzles. Add water to cover, bring to a boil, and lower heat to simmer until pork is very tender, for about 2 hours. Leave the gravy slightly watery if preferred or let the oil rise to the surface.

Wet Nan Yo Kin
GRILLED PORK RIBS

Everyone loves pork ribs. In Myanmar, we often boil them into soup with a sprinkling of cabbage leaves, but a dish of grilled ribs is far superior to any ol' soup.

SERVE as a side dish with a sauce of your choice from the "Snacks" section.

INGREDIENTS

3 1/2 pounds pork ribs
1 tablespoon dark soy sauce
1 tablespoon honey
1 tablespoon ginger juice
4 cloves garlic, peeled and crushed

1 tablespoon oil
Salt to taste

DIRECTIONS

1. Knead the pork ribs with the rest of the ingredients and let marinate overnight in the refrigerator.

2. In a pan, simmer the ribs in the marinade with enough water to cover until the oil sizzles. Drain the ribs and grill until red and crisp, brushing with the pan juices as needed.

Wet Thar Baung
STEAMED PORK

This is a delicate, sweet, meatloaf-style dish that small children love.

SERVE with plain rice, a peppery clear soup, Chicken Salad, and Balachaung with raw and blanched vegetables.

INGREDIENTS

1 1/2 pounds ground pork
3 well-beaten eggs
3 tablespoons milk
4 cloves garlic, peeled and pounded
1 teaspoon light soy sauce

Salt
Pepper
A few cabbage leaves
Chopped chives

DIRECTIONS

Line an 8-inch pan with the washed cabbage leaves. Mix all other ingredients except the chives in a bowl and transfer to the pan over the cabbage leaves. Sprinkle with the chopped chives. Steam on top of a double boiler for about 20 minutes until a knife inserted into the center comes out clean.

Wet Thar Hmyit Chin
PORK WITH PICKLED BAMBOO SHOOTS

When someone in the neighborhood is cooking Hmyit Chin and the aroma wafts over the streets, passersby can get really hungry. If not sour enough, add vinegar to taste.

SERVE with plain rice, Fried Chicken, or fresh or dried Anchovies with Dried Chillies, and Nga Pi Htaung grilled shrimp paste.

INGREDIENTS

1 pound pork belly, cut into 1-inch strips
1 pound pickled bamboo shoots, squeezed dry
2 tablespoons oil
1/4 teaspoon turmeric powder
1/4 teaspoon sweet paprika

3 onions, peeled and pounded
4 cloves garlic, peeled and pounded
1 tablespoon fish sauce
4 cups water
Salt

DIRECTIONS

1. Knead the pork with the turmeric powder and very little salt and and set aside for 10 minutes.

2. Soak the pickled bamboo shoots in water for 1 hour and drain. Cut into finger-length strips. Mix all the ingredients together, kneading well, and place the pot on heat. Stir a few times and when oil sizzles, add 5 cups water, lower heat, and simmer until the pork is very tender, about 1 hour.

Wet Thani Chet
GLOSSY RED PORK

The trick to a good pork dish is to get it really tender. A proverb states that pork is the best of meats, and good health aside, it is the most delicious. At up-country feasts such as ceremonies for novitiation or weddings, it carries great prestige to be able to serve pork curry with pieces "big as a fist." (Pork trotters can be cooked the same way.)

SERVE with clear peppery soup with gourd, Green Mango Salad, and Mandalay Nga Pi Chet shrimp paste relish with raw and blanched vegetables.

INGREDIENTS

1 1/2 pounds pork rump with skin
2 tablespoons dark soy sauce
1 tablespoon ginger juice
4 tablespoons oil
3 tablespoons sugar

1 onion, peeled and pounded
4 cloves garlic, peeled and pounded
1 cup hot water
8 whole peeled shallots

DIRECTIONS

1. Wash and cut the pork into large chunks. Prick all over with a fork and knead well with the soy sauce, ginger juice, and salt. Set aside for 2 hours in the refrigerator.

2. Keep some hot water on hand. In a wok, heat the oil and sugar and cook until the sugar turns a glossy dark red. As soon as it does, add the marinated pork, 1 cup hot water, and the pounded onion and garlic and stir to incorporate the seasonings with the pork and oil.

3. Add water to cover, lower heat, and simmer about 2 hours until the pork is very tender, adding water as needed. Stir gently a few times as the meat cooks to prevent sticking.

4. Add the shallots when just a little liquid remains. Remove pot from heat when the oil rises to the surface. The pork should be a glossy red and very tender, and the shallots almost translucent.

Bai U Hin
EGG CURRY

We prefer duck eggs to chicken as they have a richer taste and color, but chicken eggs will do just as well.

SERVE with plain rice, Thick Vegetable and Chickpea Soup, Shrimp Paste Salad, and Nga Yoke Thee Hsar Htaung roasted dried chilli relish with raw and blanched vegetables.

INGREDIENTS

4 eggs
1/2 cup oil
1/8 teaspoon turmeric powder
2 onions, peeled and pounded
3 cloves garlic, peeled and pounded

2 ripe tomatoes, chopped finely
¼ teaspoon sweet paprika
1 teaspoon fish sauce
Salt to taste
4 green chillies, crushed and stems and seeds removed, or ½ teaspoon garam masala

DIRECTIONS

1. Boil enough water to cover eggs. Slide in the eggs carefully and boil uncovered for 7 minutes. Stir gently to keep the yolks in the center. Cool immediately under running water and peel the eggs.

2. Heat the oil with the turmeric powder and fry the whole peeled hard-boiled eggs until the surface turns golden and crispy all over. Drain and cut into halves.

3. Leave about 3 tablespoons oil in the pan and sauté the pounded onions and garlic for 1 minute. When fragrant, add the sweet paprika and tomatoes and cook until the tomatoes are softened.

4. Place the eggs cut-side down in the gravy, add the fish sauce and salt to taste, and cook until oil sizzles. Stir in either the garam masala or the green chillies.

Soups

Soups are sipped throughout the meal and come in four basic forms: the sour soups with lots of vegetables; the clear soups with a sprinkling of leaves added just before serving; the creamy lentil soups; and the thick, almost stewlike dishes that often can be the only accompaniment to plain rice. These stews are simply delicious, rich with beans and vegetables and flavored with a dash of tamarind to add a lively note to the harmony of tastes. They are often cooked the day before so that the flavors mingle and mature.

Chin Yay
SOUR SOUPS

Sour soups are the mainstay of most Myanmar meals. With a good Chin Yay a person can easily polish off three plates of rice.

BASIC STOCK INGREDIENTS

1 tablespoon oil

1/8 teaspoon turmeric powder

1 onion, peeled and chopped

3 cloves garlic, peeled and chopped

1/4 teaspoon sweet paprika

3 tablespoons pounded dried shrimp

3 pieces of fish or 3 small fish heads

1 teaspoon shrimp paste dissolved in a little water

1 tablespoon fish sauce

6 cups water

3 tablespoons tamarind paste dissolved in a little warm water

Salt to taste

SUGGESTED LEAVES AND VEGETABLES, ENOUGH TO MAKE A THICK SOUP

1/4 of a gourd or 6 medium daikons (white radishes), cut into thick slices

14 ounces tomatoes, roughly chopped, in which case leave out the tamarind paste

5 ounces (4 cups) water spinach or other edible leaves

DIRECTIONS

Heat the oil with the turmeric powder and sauté the chopped onion and garlic until fragrant. Add the sweet paprika, dried shrimp, fish pieces or fish heads, and the shrimp paste mixture and cook until oil sizzles. Add water and fish sauce and bring to a boil, lower heat, and simmer until the soup is reduced by 1 cup. Sieve out the bones. Stir in the tamarind paste and salt to taste. Add leaves to the boiling stock just a few minutes before serving, or earlier for vegetables.

Pei Hin
CREAMY BEAN SOUPS

Dried beans and pulses of all sizes and tastes make up a good part of Myanmar meals. We love them fried as snacks, made into salads, boiled soft and dribbled with oil, and best of all, in smooth, comforting soups. Some of the harder beans such as chickpeas need to be soaked overnight.

INGREDIENTS FOR BASIC METHOD

1 cup dried beans, soaked overnight if needed
1 small onion, peeled and sliced
1 tablespoon oil
Salt

DIRECTIONS

1. Sauté the onion slices in oil and when fragrant, add the drained washed or presoaked beans and 6 cups water. Add salt to taste and simmer until the beans are soft, adding more water as needed. With chickpeas, you should whiz half of the boiled beans in a blender to get a smoother soup or just mash the boiling peas with the back of a spoon.

2. Adding 2 crushed lemongrass heads and 4 slices of ginger to a thick chickpea soup makes for an exotic taste. Remove lemongrass and ginger before serving.

Hin Gar and Hin Cho
CLEAR SOUPS, WITH OR WITHOUT PEPPER

Hin Gar literally means "bitter soup" but it is not bitter, just a clear soup with lots of pepper. It is considered good for nursing mothers. Hin Cho has a little pepper or none. Both have various vegetables and leaves in the stock, but not as much as the sour soups.

INGREDIENTS FOR BASIC STOCK

2 tablespoons pounded dried shrimps or 1 small catfish, cleaned and grilled
4 cloves garlic, peeled and crushed
1 tablespoon fish sauce
6 cups water

1/8 teaspoon baking soda, aka soda bicarbonate (only for green leaves)
Salt to taste
Pepper

SUGGESTED LEAVES AND VEGETABLES FOR CLEAR SOUPS

1/8 of a gourd, peeled and sliced thinly (lots of pepper)

4 napa cabbage leaves in narrow shreds (lots of pepper)
1 cup pumpkin, pea, or gourd tendrils; first peel away filament from stalks (with pepper)
10 drumstick fruits, grilled and the flesh scraped with a spoon (with pepper)
1 cup drumstick leaves (with pepper)
1 cup spinach or water spinach leaves (with pepper)
1 cup glass noodles, presoaked (with pepper)
10 pumpkin or zucchini flowers, whole (with pepper)
1 cup julienned bamboo shoots and 1 cup small whole shrimps (no pepper)
1 cup roselle leaves for a tart, clear soup (no pepper)
1 cup tender tamarind leaves for a tart, clear soup (no pepper)

DIRECTIONS

Boil all the ingredients together until 5 cups remain. Sieve out the solids and bring to a boil again before serving.

NOTES:

Vegetables may need more cooking time than the leaves, which should remain green. For this, we often add 1/8 teaspoon of baking soda to the soup stock.

Some cooks do not add the leaves to the boiling soup in the pot but put the shredded leaves in the soup bowls first and pour boiling-hot stock over them.

Thee Zone Pei Hin
THICK VEGETABLE AND CHICKPEA SOUP

This thick soup is almost a stew. When served with plain rice it is so satisfying we often do not need any other curry. By not using salt fish or fish sauce, it can be a vegetarian dish. It tastes creamier without the tamarind paste.

INGREDIENTS

2 tablespoons oil

1/4 teaspoon turmeric powder

1 onion, peeled and pounded

4 cloves garlic, peeled and pounded

1 1/2 square inches salted dried fish, soaked for 1 hour and cut into cubes (optional)

1 cup chickpeas, soaked overnight and boiled until soft

6 cups water

1 small segment of gourd, peeled and cut into cubes

1 small potato, peeled and cut in half

1 eggplant, cut into cubes

3 drumstick fruits, outer skin lightly scraped and cut into 1-inch lengths

4 lady's fingers, aka okra, cut into thirds

1 tablespoon tamarind paste softened in a little water (optional)

Salt

1/2 teaspoon garam masala (optional)

DIRECTIONS

1. Cut the vegetables in almost equal sizes, wash, and drain.

2. Heat the oil with the turmeric powder and sauté the pounded onions and garlic for about 2 minutes. Add the salted fish cubes and the boiled chickpeas and cook, stirring for 2 more minutes. Use very little salt or none if salted dried fish is used.

3. Add 6 cups of water and bring to a boil without covering pot until about 5 cups remain.

4. Add the cubed vegetables, putting in the gourd and potato first, and then the eggplant, drumstick fruit, and lady's fingers. Stir in the tamarind paste and simmer. When the soup is thick, stir in the garam masala.

Kyet Pyoke Shauk Ywet
CHICKEN BROTH WITH LIME LEAVES

This is one of the most delicious soups and probably the easiest to make.

INGREDIENTS

5 cups chicken broth made from free-range chicken bones and 3 cloves garlic, peeled and chopped

1 teaspoon fish sauce

Salt

5 kaffir lime leaves, shredded very thinly, like threads

DIRECTIONS

Bring the broth to a boil with fish sauce and salt to taste and ladle into serving bowls. Sprinkle with the shredded kaffir lime leaves and serve at once.

Pei Ni Lay Hin Cho
RED LENTIL SOUP

Myanmar produces a great variety of beans, pulses, and lentils. With dried lentils, salted dried fish, and the abundant fresh fish and vegetables, our meals are already full of nutrition without red meat or dairy products. Red lentils taste better than yellow Pei War Lay of the same size.

INGREDIENTS

1 tablespoon oil
1 small onion, peeled and sliced
1/2 cup red lentils, washed and drained
1/2 cup soaked glass noodles
6 cups water

Salt
1 tablespoon fried onion slices ("Useful Information")
1/2 tablespoon onion oil (·ditto·)

DIRECTIONS

Heat the oil and sauté the onion slices for 1 minute. Add the lentils, salt to taste, and water, and boil uncovered until lentils have dissolved, about 20 minutes. As the lentils boil, lower heat and remove scum that rises. When they are soft, about 15 minutes into the cooking process, mash the lentils against the side of the pot with the back of a spoon. Add the glass noodles and turn off heat. Let the soup simmer for 2 minutes. To serve, ladle into bowls and garnish with the fried onion slices and the onion oil.

Ngar Zabalin Hin Cho
FISH AND LEMONGRASS SOUP

This is so refreshing on the palate due to the lemongrass and lime juice, and excellent on a chilly day because of the green chillies.

INGREDIENTS

6 cups rich fish stock made from scratch
2 heads lemongrass, crushed
2 slices ginger
3 green chillies, crushed roughly and stems and seeds removed

Salt or fish sauce
1 onion, peeled, sliced, soaked in water, and squeezed dry just before serving
3 tablespoons chopped coriander
Lime wedges

DIRECTIONS

Boil the fish stock with the lemongrass and ginger until about 5 cups remain. Sieve out the solids. Add salt or fish sauce to taste. Serve hot and garnished with green chillies, chopped coriander, onion slices squeezed dry, and a squeeze of lime juice.

Boo Thee Kyaw Chet
THICK SWEET GOURD SOUP

This is a sweet, rich soup and somehow the fried fish brings out all the flavor of the gourd.

INGREDIENTS

10 1/2 ounces fish fillets, cut into 3/4-inch cubes

Oil for deep-frying

1 tablespoon oil

1/8 teaspoon turmeric powder

2 onions, peeled and sliced

4 cloves garlic, peeled and crushed

1/2 of a gourd, peeled and cut into ¾-inch chunks

1 tablespoon fish sauce

6 cups water

Salt

3 tablespoons chopped coriander

DIRECTIONS

1. Rub the fish cubes with a little salt to taste and deep-fry until golden and crisp on the outside.

2. Heat 1 tablespoon oil with the turmeric powder and sauté the onions and garlic for 1 minute. Add the gourd, fried fish, fish sauce, and water and bring to a boil. Lower heat and simmer until the gourd is very soft and almost mushy. Add salt to taste. Serve sprinkled with the chopped coriander.

Vegetables

Fresh vegetables are abundantly available all year round and in the countryside, edible leaves are easily gathered from meadows or from one's fence. On religious days or on the weekday of one's birth, some Buddhists like to be vegetarian and there's no difficulty preparing a variety of dishes. A farmer's meal may often be just plain rice, a hot, fish-based soup chock-full of leafy greens, some fried fish, and a large bowl of hot and salty relish with a variety of raw vegetables. Farmers work all year round on this fare, getting their nutrition from the fish or shrimp paste and the vitamins from the freshly gathered greens.

Pyaungbu Htaung Kyaw
CREAMY CORN

This is a light dish to soothe our palates when we are overcome with rich curries.

INGREDIENTS

8 ears of fresh corn
3 tablespoons oil
1 onion, peeled and sliced
3 tablespoons milk

Salt to taste
1/4 teaspoon sugar
Pepper

DIRECTIONS

1. Cut the kernels off the cob by slicing thinly downward as you hold the cob upright. If the cut kernels are too big, pound or grind 1/4 of them to make the dish smoother. Mix again with the cut kernels.

2. Heat the oil and sauté the onion slices for 1 minute. Add all the other ingredients with 1 cup water and cook, stirring often, until oil sizzles and the corn is tender.

Bon Lone Thee A Sar Thut
STUFFED SNAKE GOURD

Bon Lone Thee or Pei Lin Mwe Thee is a long gourd. It is hollow and its taste blends well with the meat stuffed inside. To test the freshness of one, shake it gently while holding one end; it should be flexible.

INGREDIENTS

1 Bon Lone Thee, about 20 inches long
10 1/2 ounces ground lean pork
1 onion, peeled and pounded
4 cloves garlic, peeled and pounded
2 teaspoons light soy sauce

4 tablespoons oil
1 onion, peeled and sliced
Salt

DIRECTIONS

1. Scrape the thin skin of the Bon Lone Thee. Trim off the ends and cut into 3-inch lengths. Scoop out the seeds and membranes with a thin knife, twisting the blade to clean the insides really well.

2. Combine the ground pork, pounded onion and garlic, and the light soy sauce and fry in 2 tablespoons of oil until the ground pork is cooked. Stuff the pork into the hollow Bon Lone Thee sections.

3. Heat the remaining 2 tablespoons oil and sauté the sliced onions for 1 minute, then add the Bon Lone Thee with water to cover. Add salt to taste and simmer until oil sizzles. Bon Lone Thee should be simmered long enough to remove its "fresh" smell.

Hmo Gazun Ywet Kyaw
STIR-FRIED WATER SPINACH WITH MUSHROOMS

Gazun Ywet, aka morning glory or water spinach, is a hardy and abundant vegetable that grows in water. We eat many kind of hmo, mushrooms, and the best ones are found wild with the first showers of monsoon. The blanching process keeps the water spinach green.

INGREDIENTS

14 ounces or 2 bunches water spinach, cut into 4-inch lengths, washed, and drained

1/4 teaspoon baking soda, aka soda bicarbonate

3 tablespoons oil

1 small onion, sliced thinly

1 cup mushrooms, cleaned and quartered

1/4 teaspoon light soy sauce

3 cloves garlic, peeled and chopped finely

Salt to taste

DIRECTIONS

1. Boil a pot of water with ¼ teaspoon baking soda and quickly blanch the water spinach and drain. Squeeze out gently any excess water. Set aside.

2. Heat 3 tablespoons oil in a pan and sauté the onion slices. Add the mushrooms with the light soy sauce and stir-fry until the mushrooms are cooked. Add the chopped garlic, the water spinach, and salt to taste. Stir well. Remove pan from heat and serve at once.

A Nyar Pei Gyi Chet
UP-COUNTRY BUTTER BEANS

Up-country people grow a lot of excellent beans and love them. They have fabulous beans with names like "Maung Ma Khaw Pei," "So-good-you-won't-share-it-with-your-brother."

INGREDIENTS

1 tablespoon oil

1 onion, peeled and sliced roughly

2 cups butter beans, soaked overnight and the skins squeezed off

Salt

Water

Several tender sprigs of Hsoo Poke Ywet (Acacia pennata Wild) (optional)

1 tablespoon fried onion slices ("Useful Information")

DIRECTIONS

1. Heat the oil. and sauté the onion slices for 1 minute, then add the butter beans and salt, stirring a few times. Add enough water to cover by 2 inches. Bring to a boil and immediately reduce heat and simmer. Shake the pot now and then to prevent sticking, even if you are using a nonstick pan, as this also evens out the beans.

2. When the beans are tender and the oil sizzles, top with some tender Hsoo Poke Ywet. Transfer to dish and garnish with the fried onion slices.

Kha Yan Thee Hnut
STUFFED EGGPLANT

Small and slender Japanese eggplants are the best. Many Buddhists turn vegetarian on special religious holidays, and eggplants make a good curry. This recipe without meat is a good example.

INGREDIENTS

6 eggplants
10 1/2 ounces lean ground pork or 1/2 cup pounded dried shrimp
1 onion, peeled and chopped
Fish sauce
1/3 cup oil
1/8 teaspoon turmeric powder

1 onion, peeled and sliced
3 cloves garlic, peeled and chopped
1/4 teaspoon shrimp paste softened in a little water
1/4 teaspoon sweet paprika
Salt

DIRECTIONS

1. Cut the eggplants into quarters from the end up to just near the stem. Cut away the seeded part from each quarter and pound or grind the seeds with the ground pork or dried shrimp and the chopped onion, seasoning it with fish sauce. Place the mixture between the cut quarters of the eggplants and tie loosely with string so that the stuffing stays in place.

2. Heat the oil with the turmeric powder. Sauté the onion slices for 1 minute and add the chopped garlic. Fry for 1/2 minute more and add the shrimp paste and the sweet paprika. Immediately add the eggplants, salt to taste, and enough water to cover. As they cook, turn over the eggplants gently, reduce heat, and simmer until oil sizzles. Remove strings before serving.

Hmyit Pazun Hsait Kyaw
BAMBOO SHOOTS WITH SHRIMPS

Bamboo grows quickly in the monsoon and there is nothing as delicious as bamboo shoots fresh from the woods. There are many varieties: the gigantic ones called Wa Boe are fantastic cooked fresh or pickled with pork. The smaller shoots are sold already boiled and julienned to be fried or made into soup. Boiled bamboo shoots make perfect accompaniments for the salty, hot relishes.

INGREDIENTS

3/4 pound bamboo shoots, boiled and
    squeezed dry
3 tablespoons oil
1/8 teaspoon turmeric powder
1 onion, peeled and sliced

5 ounces shrimps, washed and peeled
Salt

DIRECTIONS

1. Hold each boiled bamboo shoot by the thick end and pull a large needle or toothpick along its length to shred it easily into strips, turning the bamboo shoot around as you work. Finally cut away the thick end and slice it thinly.

2. Heat the oil in a wok with the turmeric powder and sauté the onion slices for 1 minute. Add the shrimps and fry until the shrimps turn pink and curl up. Add the bamboo shoots with salt to taste and fry until just dry.

Kyet Hin Gar Thee Kyaw
BITTER GOURD WITH SHRIMPS

Bitter gourd looks like a cucumber with little ridges along its length. The darker the skin the more bitter it tastes. It is used a lot in healing diets and traditional Myanmar medicine as we believe it regenerates dead cells.

INGREDIENTS

3 medium bitter gourds
1 tablespoon salt
1/4 cup oil
1/8 teaspoon turmeric powder
1 onion, peeled and sliced

5 ounces washed and peeled small shrimps or
 5 ounces pork belly, cut into thin strips
1 teaspoon light soy sauce
Salt

DIRECTIONS

1. Cut the bitter gourds in half lengthwise, scrape out all the seeds and the membrane, and then cut into thin crescents. Place in a bowl with 1 tablespoon salt and knead well. Set aside for 20 minutes, then wash several times to rid the gourds of any saltiness and bitterness.

2. Heat the oil with the turmeric powder and sauté the sliced onion for 1 minute. Add the shrimps or pork with soy sauce and fry, adding a dash of water if using pork, until oil sizzles. Add the well-squeezed bitter gourd pieces with salt to taste and a little more water and fry, stirring, until the gourds wilt.

Thee Sone Thanut
LIGHTLY PICKLED VEGETABLES

The word "lightly" here implies that the vegetables are not actually pickled but treated with tamarind paste or vinegar to change their taste. Using vinegar keeps the colors better.

INGREDIENTS

1 medium cucumber
Vinegar
Tamarind paste
Salt to taste
¼ teaspoon sugar
2 small Japanese eggplants
2 bamboo shoots
1 medium daikon

4 lady's fingers
2 carrots
4 stalks water spinach
4 long beans
Onion oil and fried onion slices ("Useful Information")
Toasted sesame seeds

DIRECTIONS

1. Cut the unpeeled cucumber in half lengthwise and cut away the soft seeded part. Slice the cucumber into thin crescents and knead with a little salt and vinegar. Wrap in a clean towel and place between two plates. Put a heavy object on the top so that the cucumber pieces are pressed. Leave for 1 hour prior to serving and squeeze out any residual liquid. They will be crunchy.

2. Boil the other vegetables separately with a ratio of 1 cup water mixed with 2 tablespoons tamarind paste or 3 tablespoons vinegar plus a little salt. Take care to retain color of the vegetables by not overcooking. Drain and immediately place in cold water. Drain again and cut into 3/4-inch cubes. Mix each vegetable including cucumber with 1/2 teaspoon of the onion oil. Garnish with sesame seeds and the fried onion slices. Place in separate piles on a large plate.

Salads

Myanmar cuisine is not complete without a side dish of a salad, and they are also eaten as snacks. When men gather to drink in the evenings, they often have a variety of salads with their beer or toddy palm wine. Myanmar people love their salads "chin-chin, ngan-ngan, sut-sut," which means sour, salty, and hot, washed down with a clear peppery soup or green tea. Of all the salads, the pickled tea leaf salad is the most popular snack in the country. The tea leaves, which have been steamed and buried to mature for six months, are washed and pounded with garlic, steeped in oil, and then served with sesame seeds, nuts, fried beans, dried fish, and fried garlic. It is considered an honorable dish and is served at all important ceremonies.

Tofu Thoke
TOFU SALAD

This tofu, made from chickpea powder, aka channa dhal, can also be deep-fried to make great finger food. See under "Snacks."

INGREDIENTS

1/2 cup raw chickpea powder (not roasted)

1 1/2 cups water

1 teaspoon salt

3 cloves garlic, peeled and pounded

3 tablespoons vinegar

2 teaspoons onion oil ("Useful Information")

Fried onion slices (-ditto-)

Roasted dried red chilli powder (-ditto-)

1/8 teaspoon fish sauce

3 tablespoons finely cut kaffir lime leaves

Salt to taste

DIRECTIONS

1. Dissolve the chickpea powder and 1 teaspoon salt in ½ cup of the water and pass the mixture through a very fine sieve, pushing down the lumps with a spoon until all of the powder is dissolved.

2. Bring to a boil 1 cup of water, lower heat, and pour in the chickpea mixture a little at a time, stirring constantly and scraping the sides and bottom of the pot with a flat-tipped spatula.

3. Keep on pouring the chickpea mixture by batches into the pot, stirring constantly until the mixture is glossy and thickens enough to almost leave the sides of the pot. To prevent burning or curdling, remove the pot from heat from time to time while stirring. When the mixture becomes very thick, pour into a lightly oiled pan of a size that allows the tofu to be at least 1 inch high. Leave to set in the refrigerator.

4. Cut the tofu into thin, 2-inch-long strips. Mix the slices gently with the seasonings, using the vinegar-garlic mixture according to taste. Garnish with the finely cut kaffir lime leaves and fried onion slices. Serve roasted dried red chilli powder on the side.

Kyet Thar Thoke
CHICKEN SALAD

INGREDIENTS

3 chicken breasts, poached and cut into strips
1 onion, peeled, sliced, soaked in water, and squeezed dry just before mixing
1 medium cucumber, cut into strips
1 large tomato, cut into thin slices
1/2 teaspoon fish sauce
Lime juice to taste

1 1/2 teaspoons onion oil ("Useful Information")
1/8 teaspoon sugar
Salt to taste
2 chopped green chillies, stems and seeds removed
2 tablespoons chopped coriander

DIRECTIONS

Apart from the coriander and green chillies, combine all the other ingredients in a bowl. Add salt to taste. Transfer to a serving dish and top with the fried onion slices. Garnish with the chopped green chillies and coriander.

Hin Nu Nwe Ywet Thoke
SPINACH SALAD

Unlike other salads, this is not dressed with lime juice or vinegar. It is what we call "A Cho Thoke," a sweet salad.

INGREDIENTS

10 1/2 ounces or 3 bunches spinach
1 firm tomato
2 teaspoons onion oil ("Useful Information")
1 teaspoon fish sauce
1 tablespoon pounded dried shrimp
1/8 teaspoon sugar

3 tablespoons coarsely pounded roasted peanuts
Salt to taste
1 tablespoon fried onion slices ("Useful Information")

DIRECTIONS

1. Pick the leaves and small stalks from the spinach and discard the thicker stalks. Blanch in boiling water, squeeze dry, and chop roughly.

2. Remove seeds from the tomato and chop into small cubes. Pat dry. Mix everything lightly and serve garnished with the fried onion slices.

Kha Yan Thee Mee Hpoke Thoke
GRILLED EGGPLANT SALAD

Grilling the eggplant over a charcoal fire may be messy but imparts a delightfully smoky flavor to the dish. The grilled eggplant can also be stir-fried with egg. Globe eggplants are the best for this recipe.

INGREDIENTS

1 large globe eggplant
2 onions, peeled, sliced, soaked in water, and
  squeezed dry just before mixing
2 teaspoons onion oil ("Useful Information")
Fried onion slices (·ditto·)

Salt to taste
Lime juice to taste (optional)

DIRECTIONS

1. Poke the eggplant with a skewer a few times all over and grill until the skin chars. You can also bake the whole, pierced eggplant in an oven for about 30 minutes at a medium-high temperature; place it on a grill stand so that the juices drip off and turn often to cook all sides. Every part must be cooked through until the flesh is soft.

2. Remove the charred skin carefully and mash the flesh in a deep bowl using a knife. Mix in the squeezed onion slices, the onion oil, and salt to taste. Squeeze in lime juice. Serve topped with the fried onion slices.

Myin Kwa Ywet Thoke
PENNYWORT SALAD

Myin Kwa Ywet, aka pennywort, has round, bright green leaves. Considered good for the kidneys, they are often dried in the shade and used as an alternative to green tea leaves. They are available in Asian groceries.

INGREDIENTS

3 cups loosely packed pennywort leaves
1 onion, peeled, sliced, soaked in water, and
   squeezed dry just before mixing
2 tablespoons dried shrimp powder ("Useful
   Information")
1/2 teaspoon fish sauce

1/8 teaspoon sugar
2 teaspoons onion oil ("Useful Information")
1 tablespoon fried onion slices (·ditto·)
2 tablespoons crushed roasted peanuts
Lime juice to taste
Salt to taste

DIRECTIONS

Wash the pennywort leaves and allow to dry. Chop roughly. In a bowl, combine all the other ingredients apart from the fried onion slices. Add salt to taste. Transfer to a serving dish and top with the fried onion slices.

Pazun Sein Thoke
RAW SHRIMP SALAD

This is a dish from the southern coastal towns, where they have abundant seafood.

INGREDIENTS

10 1/2 ounces peeled shrimps
Lime juice to almost cover the shrimps
2 onions, peeled, sliced, soaked in water, and
  squeezed dry just before mixing
1/2 teaspoon shrimp paste, grilled lightly

4 kaffir lime leaves, sliced very thinly
2 chopped green chillies, stems and seeds
  removed
1 teaspoon fish sauce
Salt to taste

DIRECTIONS

Cut the shrimps into small cubes and soak in lime juice for 20 minutes, stirring one or two times. Drain shrimp meat and mix gently but thoroughly with all the other ingredients.

Nga Hpai Thoke
FISH CAKE SALAD

This is one salad that is never absent from festive meals. It goes perfectly with Glass Noodle Soup.

INGREDIENTS

1 cup fish paste, preferably from Nga Hpai, aka featherback fish

1 onion, peeled and chopped

3 cloves garlic, peeled and chopped

1 thin slice ginger, chopped finely

Salt to taste

Oil for frying

3 leaves cabbage, julienned, kept soaked in cold water, and drained well before mixing

1 1/2 teaspoons onion oil ("Useful Information")

1 tablespoon fried onion slices (·ditto·)

1 teaspoon roasted chickpea powder (·ditto·)

1 teaspoon fish sauce

Lime juice to taste

2 chopped green chillies, stems and seeds removed

1 tablespoon chopped coriander

DIRECTIONS

Grind the fish paste, salt, chopped onion, garlic, and ginger together. Wet your hands and form the fish paste into 1-inch rounds. Fry until golden, drain, cool, and cut into thin strips. Mix the fish cake strips with the other ingredients and garnish with the coriander.

Nga Pi Thoke
SHRIMP PASTE SALAD

This is an easy dish, salad and relish in one.

INGREDIENTS

2 tablespoons shrimp paste, grilled lightly

2 onions, peeled, sliced, soaked in water, and squeezed dry just before mixing

2 heads lemongrass, using only the innermost soft layers, sliced very thinly

1/2 teaspoon oil

1/8 teaspoon sugar

Lime juice to taste

2 chopped green chillies, stems and seeds removed

DIRECTIONS

1. Stick a flattened round of shrimp paste on a wooden spoon and let it grill close to an open flame, or to reduce the smell, pack it tightly in aluminum foil, and grill.

2. Mix all ingredients thoroughly just before serving. Garnish with the chopped green chillies.

Mon Lar U Thoke
DAIKON SALAD

Daikon is the white radish, and cut into coils for this dish looks as charming as it is delicious.

INGREDIENTS

2 medium daikons
1 teaspoon salt
1 tablespoon vinegar or lime juice
1 teaspoon fish sauce
1 1/2 teaspoons onion oil ("Useful
Information")
1 tablespoon toasted sesame seeds
1/8 teaspoon sugar
1 tablespoon dried shrimp powder ("Useful
Information")
Fried onion slices (·ditto·)

DIRECTIONS

1. Peel or scrape off the thin skin of the daikon. Place two flat boards so that a trough ¼ high up the sides of the daikon is formed. Place the tuber horizontally in the trough. Cut slantwise into thin, uniform slices all along one side. The boards will ensure that the knife does not slice through to the bottom. Flip the radish over end on end, not sideways, and cut the other side as before. Cut this way, the radish can be pulled apart like a coiled spring.

2. Knead the cut daikons with the salt and let stand for 1 hour. Wash several times over and squeeze dry. Mix with the other ingredients. Serve garnished with the fried onion slices.

Pei Daunt Shay Thoke
LONG BEAN SALAD

The unique way of cutting the long beans gives them a crunchy texture.

INGREDIENTS

10 1/2 ounces long beans
Baking soda, aka soda bicarbonate
1 teaspoon fish sauce
4 tablespoons coarsely pounded roasted peanuts
1/8 teaspoon sugar

Lime juice to taste
Salt to taste
1 1/2 teaspoons onion oil ("Useful Information")
Fried onion slices (·ditto·)

DIRECTIONS

Cut the long beans along their length with scissors so that you get long strips. Cut again into 4·inch lengths. Boil with a little baking soda to retain greenness and squeeze out all liquid. Do not discard seeds. Mix the beans and seeds with the other ingredients and serve garnished with the fried onion slices.

Kha Yan Chin Thee Thoke
TOMATO SALAD

This is a salad quick to prepare and different in taste from tomato salads of the West, due to the fish sauce!

INGREDIENTS

5 ripe, firm tomatoes, sliced thinly, seeds removed, and patted dry

1 onion, peeled, sliced, soaked in water, and squeezed dry just before mixing

1/2 tablespoon roasted chickpea powder ("Useful Information")

1 1/2 teaspoons onion oil (-ditto-)

1/2 teaspoon fish sauce

1/8 teaspoon sugar

3 tablespoons roughly chopped coriander

1 teaspoon chopped green chillies

Salt to taste

DIRECTIONS

In a bowl, combine all the ingredients apart from the coriander and green chillies. Add salt to taste. Mix gently. Transfer to a serving dish and top with the chopped green chillies and coriander.

Tha Yet Thee Sein Thoke
GREEN MANGO SALAD

This is a salad you can make as sour as you like or not, according to how much dried shrimp powder you use to even out the sourness. It goes very well with fatty dishes like pork or duck.

INGREDIENTS

2 green mangoes, peeled and soaked in water
   15 minutes
1 onion, peeled and sliced thinly
1 teaspoon onion oil ("Useful Information")
1 1/2 teaspoons roasted chickpea powder
   (·ditto·)
2 teaspoons dried shrimp powder (·ditto·)

1/4 teaspoon sugar
Salt to taste
1 chopped green chilli, stems and seeds
   removed
1 teaspoon fried onion slices ("Useful
   Information")

DIRECTIONS

Scrape the peeled green mango into long, thin strips. Mix thoroughly and gently with the other ingredients. Serve garnished with the fried onion slices.

Shaut Thee Thoke
CITRUS SALAD

We use a bigger kind of kaffir lime for this, but pomelo or grapefruit can be substituted. We often serve this with Glass Noodle Soup.

INGREDIENTS

1 large kaffir lime or 1 pomelo or 2 grapefruits

4 leaves cabbage, julienned

1 onion, peeled, sliced, soaked in water, and squeezed dry just before mixing

1 teaspoon shrimp paste, lightly grilled

1/4 teaspoon sugar

1 teaspoon roasted chickpea powder ("Useful Information")

1 tablespoon dried shrimp powder (·ditto·)

1 teaspoon chopped green chillies or roasted dried red chilli powder ("Useful Information")

1 tablespoon chopped coriander

DIRECTIONS

Remove all of the membrane and skin carefully from the kaffir lime, pomelo or grapefruit segments and mix lightly with the other ingredients. Garnish with the coriander. It is best to prepare the fruit just before serving.

Pei Zaung Lya Thee Thoke
WINGED BEAN SALAD

Winged beans are a good source of protein. When just lightly blanched they retain their bright green color and crisp texture. They are usually served with relishes but, combined with the sweetness of prawns in a salad, make a great side dish to any meal.

INGREDIENTS

15 winged beans
7 ounces shelled prawns
1 tablespoon toasted sesame seeds
1 teaspoon onion oil ("Useful Information")
1 teaspoon roasted chickpea powder (·ditto·)

Salt to taste
Lime juice to taste

DIRECTIONS

1. Lightly blanch winged beans and soak in cold water. Drain well and cut into thin slices.

2. Boil the peeled prawns in a little water with salt to taste until the prawns turn pink. Do not overcook. Cool and chop into ½-inch cubes.

3. To serve, mix the winged beans and prawns with all the other ingredients.

Jinn Thoke
GINGER SALAD

The national dish of Myanmar is the pickled tea leaf served with nuts and beans. However, as pickled tea leaf is not usually available outside of Myanmar, here is its close cousin the ginger salad. The two are usually served together as an after-meal snack. The modern housewives have found that ginger salad makes a tantalizing side dish for roast duck. The amounts for the other ingredients are the same for tea leaf.

INGREDIENTS

1/2 cup pickled ginger, julienned (Japanese pickled ginger will do)
Oil for frying
1/2 cup peeled garlic, cut into thin rounds
1/2 cup roasted peanuts
1/2 cup fried chickpeas
1/2 cup toasted sesame seeds

1/2 cup toasted pumpkin seeds
4 tablespoons dried shrimp powder ("Useful Information") or 20 whole dried shrimps
1/2 cup deep-fried butter beans
1/4 teaspoon salt
2 teaspoons oil

DIRECTIONS

Squeeze all liquid out of the pickled ginger and julienne. Fry garlic rounds on low heat until golden and crisp. Pan-roast sesame seeds and pumpkin seeds for 1 minute each. Mix all the ingredients together or serve in separate piles.

Relishes

Even without a meat curry the Myanmar meal is adequately delicious with rice, a soup, and a good salty, hot, and sour relish. The Upper Myanmar people favor relishes made with tomatoes and shrimp paste while Southerners like it made with pickled fish. Whatever the base, it always makes a great combination with raw or blanched vegetables. Quite a number of leaves and fruits are also pickled in brine to be eaten with these piquant dips.

SUGGESTED VEGETABLES TO GO WITH RELISHES

Raw cucumbers, carrots, cubes of lime with peel, kaffir lime leaves, cabbage leaves, small green mango halves soaked in water for an hour and drained, cubes of raw onion, and lettuce leaves.

Blanched water spinach leaves, winged beans, lady's fingers, mustard greens, baby mustard greens, baby eggplants, bean sprouts, and cauliflower sprigs.

Boiled bamboo shoots and daikons.

Pickled edible leaves and shoots too numerous to mention by name.

Mandalay Nga Pi Chet
SHRIMP PASTE RELISH OF MANDALAY

My mother always cooked this herself, declaring that our cook, Ma Nyein, who was from the far south, could not come within one thousand miles of making the real thing.

INGREDIENTS

3 tablespoons oil

1/4 teaspoon turmeric powder

1 onion, peeled and pounded

3 cloves garlic, peeled and pounded

1/4 teaspoon sweet paprika

1 tablespoon shrimp paste softened in a little water

6 ripe tomatoes, chopped finely

1 tablespoon tamarind paste softened in a little water

3 tablespoons dried shrimp powder ("Useful Information")

5 green chillies, crushed lightly and stems and seeds removed

Fish sauce to taste

3 tablespoons chopped coriander

DIRECTIONS

1. Heat the oil with the turmeric powder and sauté the onion and garlic for 1 minute. Add the sweet paprika and immediately add the softened shrimp paste and cook a few seconds. Add the tamarind paste and tomatoes. Cook with 3 tablespoons of water until the tomatoes are soft.

2. Add the dried shrimp powder and the green chillies and cook with fish sauce to taste until oil sizzles again. Sprinkle with the chopped coriander and remove pan from heat.

Nga Pi Yay
PICKLED FISH RELISH

Nga Pi Yay is made from pickled fish, also known as fermented fish paste. If pickled fish is not available, you can make it farmers' style by substituting it with shrimp paste boiled in a little water.

INGREDIENTS

2 tablespoons pickled fish paste

1/4 teaspoon turmeric powder

2 tablespoons dried shrimp powder ("Useful Information")

4 cloves garlic, grilled lightly, peeled, and pounded

3 green chillies, grilled lightly, stems removed, and pounded

DIRECTIONS

1. Thread the unpeeled cloves of garlic and the green chillies on a metal skewer and wave through flames or place on a hot plate for 1 minute and turn a few times.

2. Boil the pickled fish paste with the turmeric powder and 1 cup of water until reduced by half. Sieve out the bones. Mix with the dried shrimp powder, pounded garlic, and pounded green chillies. If you have a fish curry or fried fish, crumble in a small piece.

Balachaung
CRISPY FRIED DRIED SHRIMP

The spiciness can be adjusted. The sweeter version is great for sandwiches we make for picnics.

INGREDIENTS

1/2 cup oil

5 cloves garlic, peeled and cut into rounds of uniform thickness

1/4 teaspoon turmeric powder

1/4 teaspoon sweet paprika

1 tablespoon shrimp paste softened in a little water

1 teaspoon tamarind paste softened in a little water

1 cup dried shrimp powder ("Useful Information")

1 teaspoon sugar or to taste

3 tablespoons fried onions ("Useful Information")

DIRECTIONS

1. Heat oil with the turmeric powder and fry the garlic rounds until crisp and golden, about ½ minute. Drain, cool, and store in airtight jar.

2. In the remaining oil, stir in the sweet paprika and the dried shrimp powder. Immediately add the shrimp paste, tamarind paste, and sugar and fry, stirring until it turns golden brown. Cool, and stir in the fried onions first and then the fried garlic.

Ngan Pyar Yay Hpyaw
FISH SAUCE RELISH

Fish sauce can be eaten straight from the bottle. The boiling process is to intensify the taste. If preferred, the boiling process can be eliminated and only half the quantity of fish sauce used.

INGREDIENTS

1 cup fish sauce

1 tablespoon oil

1 teaspoon roasted dried red chilli powder ("Useful Information")

3 cloves garlic, peeled and pounded

1 tablespoon dried shrimp powder ("Useful Information")

DIRECTIONS

1. Heat the oil and fry the garlic for ½ minute and then add the dried shrimp powder. Remove the pan from heat immediately. Set aside.

2. Bring the fish sauce to a boil and simmer until about half remains. Mix in the dried-shrimp-powder-and-garlic mixture and simmer a few more seconds. Sprinkle with the roasted dried red chilli powder before serving.

Kha Yan Chin Thee Pan Htway Hpyaw
GRILLED TOMATO RELISH

Pan Htway Hpyaw is a relish with a smoky flavor. Some prefer boiling the tomatoes to grilling them.

INGREDIENTS

6 ripe tomatoes
4 green chillies
1 onion, peeled, sliced, soaked in water, and squeezed dry just before serving
1 tablespoon fish sauce

1 teaspoon dried shrimp powder ("Useful Information")
Salt
4 tablespoons coriander, chopped roughly

DIRECTIONS

Thread the tomatoes and the green chillies on a metal skewer and grill over a charcoal fire until the skins are almost charred. Peel, remove seeds, and mash the tomatoes. Remove stems and seeds from the grilled chillies and pound. Mix with the other ingredients.

Nga Pi Lainmar
THE WELL-BEHAVED PICKLED FISH

No one can explain the name, but nevertheless it is a great relish. Perhaps cooking the Nga Pi tamed it!

INGREDIENTS

2 tablespoons oil
1 small onion, peeled and pounded
3 cloves garlic, peeled and pounded
1 tablespoon shrimp paste softened in a little water

1 tablespoon tamarind paste dissolved in a little water
1 tablespoon roasted dried red chilli powder ("Useful Information")
1 tablespoon dried shrimp powder (·ditto·)

DIRECTIONS

Heat the oil and sauté the pounded onion and garlic for 1 minute. Add the softened shrimp paste and fry a few seconds. Add the tamarind paste dissolved in a little water and let cook 2 minutes, then stir in the dried shrimp powder and the roasted dried red chilli powder.

Pazun Hsait Nga Yoke Thee Hpyaw
SPICY SHRIMP RELISH

This is hot enough to burn your throat. It goes well with tiny pieces of cut lime, peel and all.

INGREDIENTS

1 teaspoon oil
1/8 teaspoon turmeric powder
1 small onion, peeled and sliced
3 cloves garlic, peeled and pounded
2 tablespoons fish sauce

1 cup of grilled and shelled small shrimps, chopped roughly
8 green chillies, grilled lightly, stems removed, and pounded

DIRECTIONS

1. Thread the green chillies on a metal skewer and wave through flames to grill them.

2. Heat the oil with the turmeric powder and sauté the onion slices for 1 minute. Add the garlic and in 1/2 minute, add the shrimps, fish sauce, and the green chillies. Remove from heat when the shrimps turn pink.

Nga Pi Htaung
GRILLED SHRIMP PASTE

A word of warning: grilling the shrimp paste can flavor the whole neighborhood, so it's best to first wrap it in foil and seal the edges tightly. Just putting this package on a hot plate and turning it once or twice is enough to cook the shrimp paste.

INGREDIENTS

4 green chillies, grilled lightly, stems removed
2 tablespoons dried shrimp powder ("Useful
   Information")
3 tablespoons shrimp paste, grilled lightly
1/2 teaspoon oil

Lime juice

DIRECTIONS

Thread the green chillies on a metal skewer and wave through flames. Pound the dried shrimp powder and grilled chillies together and when well mixed, add the grilled shrimp paste and pound again. Dribble with oil. Serve with a liberal squeeze of lime juice.

Nga Yoke Thee Hsar Htaung
ROASTED DRIED CHILLI RELISH

Nga Yoke Thee Hsar Htaung literally means "chillies pounded with salt." Although a simple and cheap relish, it graces the tables of every level of society.

INGREDIENTS

1/4 cup roasted dried red chilli powder
   ("Useful Information")
5 cloves garlic, grilled lightly and peeled
   (·ditto·)
Salt to taste

2 teaspoons peanut oil
Lime juice

DIRECTIONS

1. Thread the unpeeled cloves of garlic on a metal skewer and wave through flames or place on a hot plate for 1/2 minute and turn a few times.

2. Pound the chilli powder, grilled garlic, and salt and pile the mixture on a plate. Dribble with oil and serve with a squeeze of lime juice.

Rice

Rice is the staple of the country, eaten plain or made into noodles or sweets. In a Buddhist household, the first spoonfuls in the morning are placed on the household shrine and after that, into the bowls of the monks who come to stand silently in front of the house on their morning alms rounds. At meals, the oldest person present must be served first with the rice, and no one else is permitted to eat until this elder has done so.

One must not chatter while eating, nor, worst of all offenses, sing. For this sin you will grow up to marry someone as old as a grandparent. Step on a grain of rice without an apology and the Rice Ghost will give you a nightmare. Most Myanmar will not eat beef, as bulls are used in plowing rice fields and thus indirectly they supply our food. Such are the etiquettes and beliefs surrounding rice, our source of life.

Htamin Yay Khan
PLAIN RICE

Htamin means both rice and the meal itself. Yay Khan means to cook until the water evaporates. It is easiest to use a rice cooker for all the recipes here, but if you do not have one, below is a foolproof method. The only thing is that you need to watch the clock.

To use a rice cooker, wash the rice, drain well, and cook with the same ratio of water as below.

INGREDIENTS

2 cups rice
3 cups water

DIRECTIONS

1. Wash the rice, pouring out the water three or four times, finally draining well. Place in a pot with 3 cups water and boil uncovered on high heat until it bubbles and water thickens. Cook for 1 minute, then lower heat to medium. Stir quickly once and let simmer for about 3 minutes until the surface is dry and holes appear.

2. Instantly turn heat to the lowest position and cover tightly, or place two layers of paper towels between the pot and the cover. Cook for exactly 10 minutes and then turn the heat off, but do not remove pot from the heat or take off the cover. Allow to cook for a further 10 minutes.

Ohn Htamin
COCONUT RICE

This rich dish is served on special occasions and was a favorite rice dish of the last royal court.

SERVE with Chicken Curry, a clear soup, Daikon Salad, and Mandalay Nga Pi Chet shrimp paste relish with raw and blanched vegetables.

INGREDIENTS

1 tablespoon oil
2 cups rice, washed and drained
1 1/2 cups coconut cream + 1 1/2 cups water to make 3 cups of liquid
2 onions, quartered

1/2 teaspoon salt
1 teaspoon sugar
2 tablespoons fried onion slices ("Useful Information")

DIRECTIONS

1. Heat the oil and sauté the onions for 1 minute. Add the drained rice and fry 1 more minute. Stir in salt, sugar, and the mixture of coconut cream and water. Boil uncovered on high heat until it bubbles and water thickens. Cook for 1 minute, then lower heat to medium. Simmer for about 3 minutes until the surface is dry and holes appear.

2. Instantly turn heat to the lowest position and cover tightly. Cook for exactly 10 minutes and then turn the heat off, but do not remove pot from the heat or take off the cover. Allow to cook for a further 10 minutes. Serve the rice sprinkled with the fried onions.

Hsan Pyoke
RICE PORRIDGE

Perfect for recuperating patients or children, or just as a light supper, rice gruel fragrant with onion oil and green onions is also great comfort food.

SERVE with hard-boiled salted duck eggs and crisp-fried Chinese sausage (both under "Useful Information").

INGREDIENTS

1 1/2 cups cooked rice

2 cups water

4 cups rich chicken broth made from scratch with 4 cloves crushed garlic and 1 teaspoon julienned ginger

14 ounces chicken breast, cut into small cubes

1 tablespoon light soy sauce

Onion oil or garlic oil ("Useful Information")

4 teaspoons fried onion slices (·ditto·)

1/2 cup chopped chives or green onions

Salt

Pepper

DIRECTIONS

1. Put the cooked rice and water in a blender and whiz until smooth. Transfer to a pot and boil uncovered with the broth and chicken pieces until the chicken is cooked through and the rice has softened, about 30 minutes. Add salt to taste.

2. Serve garnished with fried onion slices, chives or green onions, and a dribble of onion oil. Add pepper if desired. Set out plates of light soy sauce to add as preferred, and quartered hard-boiled salted duck eggs and slices of Chinese sausages.

Sar Daw Pei Byoke Htamin Kyaw
FRIED RICE WITH GARDEN PEAS

Sar Daw Pei peas are literally "Peas for Royalty," but they have always been the main breakfast dish of the masses. They are small brown dried peas that when soaked produce a tiny curly sprout like a miniature piggy's tail. Each pea also has a small black eye, making it as amusing to look at as it is versatile to cook. They are sold ready-steamed and mostly eaten with Indian naan, fried with rice, or even fried on their own as a side dish.

SERVE with Fried Chicken (see under "Snacks"),

INGREDIENTS

5 cups cooked rice, cooled completely

1/2 teaspoon salt

3 tablespoons oil

1/4 teaspoon turmeric powder

1 onion, peeled and sliced

1 cup black-eyed peas, boiled and well drained

DIRECTIONS

1. Mix the cold rice with the salt.

2. In a large wok heat the oil with the turmeric powder and sauté the onions for 1 minute.

3. Add the rice and fry, stirring often, for about 7 minutes until the rice is almost dry. Add the boiled peas and fry 1 minute more. Serve warm.

Dun Pauk
BYRANI RICE

Our Byrani was created by the familes of immigrant Indians who settled in Myanmar a few generations ago. It tastes quite different from the same dish of other countries. It is an excellent one-dish meal, where the meat, gravy, and rice are all cooked in one pot.

This recipe is more complicated than other rice dishes so it is better to use the rice cooker.

SERVE with a clear soup of roselle, mango pickles, and a simple relish of raw onions mixed with salt, crushed mint, vinegar, and sugar.

INGREDIENTS

4 large pieces of chicken, e.g., 2 whole legs and 2 halves of breast

1/4 cup yogurt

Salt to taste

1 1/2 tablespoons Curry Powder for Byrani (see subsequent recipe)

5 tablespoons ghee, aka clarified butter1 tablespoon oil

2 cups rice, washed and well drained

3 1/2 cups water

5 tablespoons fried onion slices ("Useful Information")

1/2 teaspoon saffron, crushed to a powder and steeped for 3 hours with 2 tablespoons warm water scented with a few drops of rose essence

2 tablespoons each raisins, cashew nuts, and green peas

DIRECTIONS

1. Prick the chicken pieces all over and then knead well with the yogurt, salt, and the Byrani curry powder. Let marinate 3 hours in the refrigerator.

2. Heat 1 tablespoon oil and 5 tablespoons ghee. Add the chicken plus its marinade with ½ cup of water and sauté until the chicken is nearly cooked through and the oil sizzles, about 4 minutes.

3. In the rice cooker, place the chicken pieces at the bottom, cover with a layer of the well-drained rice, and sprinkle with some of the gravy from the chicken. Add another layer of rice and sprinkle with 1 tablespoon crisp fried onions. Repeat with the rice, gravy, and fried onions. Add 3½ cups water and salt to taste, and switch on the cooker. When the liquid is almost all absorbed, quickly stir in the saffron water and the raisins, nuts, and green peas using a nonmetal ladle, taking care not to disturb the chicken pieces. Continue cooking until done.

Dun Pauk Masala
CURRY POWDER FOR BYRANI

INGREDIENTS

3 sticks cinnamon

2 pieces star anise

2 tablespoons cumin seeds

1 tablespoon caraway seeds

3 cardamom pods, crushed lightly

5 whole cloves

½ a nutmeg seed

DIRECTIONS

Pan-roast each ingredient separately over very low heat until fragrant. Grind together to a fine powder.

Pei Htaw But Htamin
LENTIL AND BUTTER RICE

This dish is often served for wedding dinners. Red lentils instead of chickpeas make a softer texture.

SERVE with Duck Vindaloo, Chicken Curry, or Chunky Beef Stew, clear soup of roselle leaves, and Balachaung with raw cucumbers.

INGREDIENTS

4 tablespoons ghee, aka clarified butter
1 tablespoon oil
1 onion, peeled and sliced
2 cups rice, washed and drained
1/4 cup red lentils, washed and well drained
3 1/4 cups water

1 small stick cinnamon
4 bay leaves, crushed
1 teaspoon salt
2 teaspoons sugar
1/4 cup green peas
2 tablespoons fried onion slices ("Useful Information")

DIRECTIONS

1. Heat the ghee and oil and sauté the onion slices for 1 minute. Add the cinnamon and bay leaves and sauté 1 minute more. Add the well-drained rice, salt, and sugar with the water. Boil uncovered on high heat until the rice bubbles. Stir in the lentils, cook for 1 minute, and lower heat to medium. Simmer for about 3 minutes until the surface is dry and holes appear.

2. Instantly turn heat to the lowest position and cover the pot tightly. Cook for exactly 10 minutes and then turn the heat off, but do not remove the pot from heat or remove the cover. Stir in the peas and allow to cook for a further 10 minutes. Remove the bay leaves and cinnamon before serving. Garnish the rice with the fried onions.

Htamin Let Thoke
RICE SALAD

Let Thoke means "mixed by hand." Exact measurements for this dish cannot be given as it is up to individual taste. The simplest rice salad is one where we mix a bowl of leftover cold rice with some fish sauce, dried shrimp powder, roasted dried red chilli powder, a little onion oil, and tamarind paste. The recipe below is more elaborate but worth all the work.

SERVE with peeled raw garlic, Fried Chicken (see under "Snacks"), and hot peppery cabbage soup.

INGREDIENTS

1/2 cup onion oil ("Useful Information")
Fried onion slices (·ditto·)
1/4 cup oil
2 tablespoons sweet paprika
2 cups cooked rice
1 cup boiled and drained glass noodles
1 cup boiled and drained egg noodles
1 cup boiled potatoes, peeled and sliced thinly
1 cup julienned green papaya, soaked in water
  and squeezed dry just before serving

1/2 cup bean sprouts, blanched
1/2 cup thinly sliced and deep-fried tofu
1/2 cup thinly sliced and deep-fried fish cakes
1/2 cup dried shrimp powder ("Useful
  Information")
1/2 cup roasted bean powder
Fish sauce
Tamarind paste softened in a little water

DIRECTIONS

1. To make chilli oil, place sweet paprika in a bowl. Heat ¼ cup of oil and when very hot, pour over the paprika. Let steep until cool and pour out, retaining the oil without the sediment.

2. Knead the cooked rice with the chilli oil and form into 4 balls. Use less oil if preferred.

3. On each plate, place 1 rice ball and as much of the other ingredients as preferred. Dribble with 2 teaspoons of the onion oil, 1 teaspoon of the fish sauce, and about 2 teaspoons of the tamarind paste and mix thoroughly by hand. Garnish with the fried onion slices and serve at once.

Noodles

The Myanmar people love noodles as a snack, as a meal, and as a convenient dish to feed the hundreds of guests that must be invited for formal celebrations. Noodles are available in many forms, including those influenced by Indian or Chinese cuisine. Most noodle shops begin to open at dawn and people going to the bazaar have their breakfast at these stalls, sitting on low stools or just standing around the boiling pot of soup. Even when they are easily available at all hours, families or groups of friends cook special noodle dishes at home "just for fun," with everyone helping out.

Mandalay Mondi
THE MYANMAR SPAGHETTI

Mondi is the native dish of Mandalay, hometown of my mother. Mandalay folks take great pride in the fact that no one outside their city knows how to make this to their taste—and no wonder, as they use a certain type of bean powder unavailable elsewhere and they tell no outsider exactly which bean it is. Living in Yangon, Mother had to use chickpea powder and found it to be a good enough substitute.

INGREDIENTS

4 servings of medium-thick, round rice
  noodles
1 1/2 pounds chicken, skinned and cut into
  3/4-inch cubes
1 teaspoon fish sauce
1/2 cup oil
1/8 teaspoon turmeric powder
2 onions, peeled and chopped finely
3 cloves garlic, peeled and chopped finely
1/3 teaspoon sweet paprika
Salt
1/2 cup onion oil ("Useful Information")
Fried onion slices (-ditto-)
1/2 cup roasted chickpea powder (-ditto-)
Fish sauce to taste

GARNISH

2 hard-boiled eggs, sliced
Chopped coriander
Lime wedges
Roasted dried red chilli powder ("Useful
  Information")
A handful dried noodles, deep-fried until puffy

SOUP

4 cups chicken broth made from scratch,
  which can be done one day ahead
3 cloves garlic, crushed
1 thin slice ginger
Chopped green onions
5 ounces fish paste, formed into small balls

DIRECTIONS

1. Knead the chicken pieces thoroughly with the fish sauce and a little salt and set aside for 10 minutes.

2. Heat the oil with the teaspoon turmeric powder and sauté the chopped onions for 1 minute. Add the chopped garlic and in about 1 minute add the sweet paprika. Almost immediately add the chicken and fry until the surface of the meat is sealed. Add the salt and fish sauce to taste. Cook with 1/2 cup water until the chicken is tender. The gravy should be a bit watery.

3. Make chicken broth from scratch with the crushed garlic, ginger slices, and enough water for four servings. This can be done one day ahead. Strain and boil again with the fish balls. Deep-fry a handful of dried noodles until puffy.

4. To serve, place noodles on each plate and add a generous ladleful of chicken with gravy, 1 teaspoon of the onion oil, 1 teaspoon of the fried onions, and 1 tablespoon of the roasted chickpea powder. Top with a few slices of hard-boiled eggs, some chopped coriander, and the puffy fried noodles. Serve the fish ball soup very hot and garnished with green onions. Lime wedges and roasted dried red chilli powder are set out for those who like it hot or with a squeeze of lime.

Monhinga
THE MYANMAR BOUILLABAISSE

Monhinga is a national noodle dish of Myanmar and especially popular in Yangon, the capital city, which lies in the southern delta where fish is abundant.

INGREDIENTS

4 servings of thin, soft rice noodles. The soft Japanese somen noodles are perfect for monhinga, but not rice vermicelli.

8-inch long stem of a banana tree. If unavailable the lack will not harm the taste of the dish, only the texture.

1 1/2 pounds catfish or other firm-fleshed fish

7 cups fish stock made from scratch with the fish, which can be done one day ahead

3 cloves garlic, peeled and crushed

2 thin slices ginger

3 heads lemongrass, crushed

1 tablespoon fish sauce

1/8 teaspoon + 1/4 teaspoon turmeric powder

1/4 cup oil

3 onions, peeled and pounded

4 cloves garlic, peeled and pounded

1 head lemongrass, sliced very thin

1 thin slice ginger, peeled and pounded

1/4 teaspoon sweet paprika

2 tablespoons fish sauce

2 tablespoons roasted chickpea powder ("Useful Information")

2 tablespoons roasted rice powder (-ditto-)

8 whole peeled small shallots

1 hard-boiled egg, peeled and sliced

3 cloves garlic + 1/2 teaspoon black pepper, pounded together

Salt

Onion oil ("Useful Information")

Fried onion slices (-ditto-)

GARNISH

5 ounces fish paste, formed into flat cakes with salt to taste and fried until golden. Cool and cut into slices.

2 hard-boiled eggs, boiled 8 minutes to keep the yolks moist. Do not peel.

Gourd fritters ("Snacks")

Chickpea fritters (-ditto-)

Roasted dried red chilli powder ("Useful Information")

Chopped coriander

Lime wedges

DIRECTIONS

1. Peel away the tough outer layers of the banana stem and when only two layers and the soft core remain, slice into 1/2-inch rounds. Soak in water for an hour, discarding the stringy sap.

2. Boil the fish with 3 cups water, 1 tablespoon fish sauce, a little salt, 1/8 teaspoon turmeric powder, 3 cloves crushed garlic, 2 thin slices ginger, and 3 crushed heads of lemongrass. Remove the fish when just done and retain the stock. Flake off and set aside the flesh in 3/4-inch pieces, taking care to remove all the bones. This step can be done one day ahead.

3. To make the stock, place the bones in a blender with 2 cups water and whiz a few seconds. Sieve out the bones and wash them with 2 cups water, then strain the liquid again, leaving the bones cleaned white. Add the liquid to the stock and bring to a boil again. Discard the lemongrass, etc. and strain the soup to make sure of removing all the bones. You may use additional fish bones such as catfish heads to make the stock richer. This step can be done one day ahead.

4. Heat 1/4 cup oil with 1/4 teaspoon turmeric powder and fry the pounded 3 onions, 4 cloves garlic, 1 head lemongrass, and 1 slice ginger for 1 minute. Stir to prevent sticking. Add the 1/4 teaspoon sweet paprika, the boiled and flaked fish pieces, and 2 tablespoons fish sauce and cook until the oil sizzles. Set aside. This step can be done one day ahead.

5. Bring the fish stock to a boil in a large pot with salt to taste. Dissolve the rice powder and chickpea powder in 1/2 cup of water and stir into the boiling stock until it thickens, adding more fish sauce if preferred. Skim off bubbles that rise to the surface.

6. Stir in the cooked fish and the banana stems. Simmer until about 6 cups of stock remain. Add the sliced hard-boiled egg and the peeled whole shallots and simmer 5 minutes more. Just before removing the pot from heat, pound 3 cloves garlic with 1/2 teaspoon black pepper and stir into the soup.

TO SERVE, place some rice noodles in a bowl and dribble with 1 teaspoon of the onion oil and a few slices of the fried onions. Ladle on a generous amount of the fish soup. Garnish with the chopped coriander and half of a hard-boiled egg. (Cut the unpeeled egg in half with a knife and scoop out with a spoon.)

Set out dishes of the fried fish-ball slices, crushed chickpea fritters, the gourd fritters cut into bite-sizes, lime wedges, and roasted dried red chilli powder for guests to serve themselves.

Mandalay Mee Shay
NOODLES WITH PICKLED TOFU

This is another noodle dish from Mandalay and one that Mother made as often as the Mondi noodles. The pickled or fermented tofu called the Cheese of the East and raw garlic are the two essential and highly pungent ingredients.

INGREDIENTS

4 servings of round, medium-sized rice noodles, boiled and drained. They should have a "bitey" texture to them.
1 pound pork belly
2 tablespoons light soy sauce
4 tablespoons starch powder
1 tablespoon rice powder
1/4 cup cold water + 1/2 cup nearly boiling water
7 ounces pork tenderloin
Salt

BATTER

2 eggs + 4 tablespoons flour + ¼ teaspoon baking powder
Oil for deep-frying

SEASONINGS

Light sweet soy sauce
1/2 cup pickled soybeans, the salty brown ones, mashed in a little warm water
2 tablespoons pickled tofu mashed in 1 teaspoon water
10 cloves garlic, peeled, pounded, and mixed with 1/4 cup vinegar

GARNISH

1 cup bean sprouts, blanched

SOUP

5 cups rich broth made from scratch, which can be done one day ahead
1/4 cup green onions, chopped
Pepper

DIRECTIONS

1. Boil the pork belly with light soy sauce until very tender. This step can be done one day ahead.

2. Mix 4 tablespoons starch powder and 1 tablespoon rice powder with ¼ cup cold water. Bring 1/2 cup water nearly to a boil, add the starch mixture slowly, and cook, stirring, until you get a thick, glue-like paste. Set aside.

3. Boil the pork tenderloin with salt to taste until tender and cut into small cubes. Dip the pork cubes in batter and fry by batches in hot oil for 2 minutes until crisp and golden. Remove from oil and drain on absorbent paper.

4. To serve, put noodles for each serving in a sieve and rinse quickly in boiling water, shake out water, and put noodles into the bowl. Top with about 1/2 teaspoon of light soy sauce, 1/2 teaspoon of the pickled soybean mixture, 1 teaspoon of the pickled tofu mixture, and 1 teaspoon of the garlic and vinegar sauce. Adjust seasonings to taste.

5. Finally add 1 heaping tablespoon of the starch and a liberal amount of the chopped boiled pork. Garnish with the sliced deep-fried pork nuggets and some blanched bean sprouts. Serve the clear broth with pepper and a sprinkling of chopped green onions.

Ohn No Khaut Swei
COCONUT NOODLES

Monhinga and Mondi are territorial dishes but in Ohn No Khaut Swei, the coconut-broth noodles, we find harmony and great taste. The Myanmar believe coconut is bad for high blood pressure, and some substitute milk or go half-half.

INGREDIENTS

4 servings of thin egg noodles
1 pound chicken, skinned and cut into ¾-inch cubes
1 teaspoon fish sauce
1/4 cup oil
1/4 teaspoon turmeric powder
2 onions, peeled and chopped finely
3 cloves garlic, peeled and chopped finely
1/2 teaspoon sweet paprika
5 ounces fish paste, formed into a flat cake with salt to taste and fried until golden. Cool and cut into cubes.
6 cups rich chicken broth made preferably from free-range chicken, which can be done one day ahead
5 tablespoons roasted chickpea powder ("Useful Information")
12 whole peeled small shallots
1 cup coconut cream
Salt

GARNISH

A handful of dried rice noodles, deep-fried until puffy
Roasted dried red chilli powder ("Useful Information")
Chopped green onions
Lime wedges
3 hard-boiled eggs, sliced into rounds
2 onions, peeled, sliced, soaked in water, and squeezed dry just before serving

DIRECTIONS

1. Knead the chicken pieces thoroughly with the fish sauce and a little salt and set aside for 10 minutes.

2. Heat the oil with turmeric powder and sauté the chopped onions for 1 minute. Add the chopped garlic, cook ½ minute more, and add the sweet paprika. Almost immediately add the chicken and cook until the surface of the meat is sealed. Add the cut fish cake and ½ cup water and simmer until oil sizzles. Set aside. This step can be done one day ahead.

3. Bring the broth to a boil. Dissolve the roasted chickpea powder in ½ cup water until smooth and add to the soup, stirring constantly until it thickens. Add salt to taste. Stir in the chicken, fish cubes, and the coconut cream. Boil hard once, lower heat, and simmer for 10 minutes. Add the shallots 5 minutes before removing the pot from the heat.

4. To serve, place a handful of noodles in a deep bowl and ladle on a generous amount of the soup. Garnish with the sliced raw onions squeezed dry, slices of hard-boiled eggs, chopped green onions, and the puffy fried noodles. Set out lime wedges, more sliced onions, and roasted dried red chilli powder to add as preferred.

Kyar Zan Chet
GLASS NOODLE SOUP

Glass noodles are made from mung beans and turn transparent when cooked. They are called Kyar Zan, which sounds like the phrase "to live long in luxury." Thus considered an auspicious dish, it is often served on New Year's and birthdays.

SERVE with Fish Cake or Citrus Salad (see under "Salads").

INGREDIENTS

6 cups rich chicken broth made preferably from free-range chicken, which can be done one day ahead

1 pound chicken breast, skinned and cut into 1-inch cubes

1 teaspoon fish sauce

Salt

2 tablespoons oil

1 onion, peeled and chopped finely

3 cloves garlic, peeled and chopped finely

1/4 teaspoon turmeric powder

1/4 teaspoon sweet paprika

20 small fish paste balls, deep-fried until golden

12 whole peeled small shallots

2 small bundles glass noodles

20 stalks dried lilies, aka golden needles, soaked and tied in a knot

1 cup tree ear mushrooms, soaked, cleaned, and drained

12 quail eggs, hard-boiled and peeled

1 bean curd sheet, cut into strips

GARNISH

Roasted dried red chilli powder ("Useful Information")

1/2 cup chopped coriander and/or 1/2 cup chopped green onions

Lime wedges

Fish sauce

Pepper

DIRECTIONS

1. Knead the chicken pieces thoroughly with the fish sauce and a little salt and set aside for 10 minutes.

2. Heat the oil with the turmeric powder and sauté the chopped onions for 1 minute. Add the chopped garlic, cook ½ minute more, and add the sweet paprika. Almost immediately add the chicken and cook until the surface of the meat is sealed. This step can be done one day ahead.

3. Transfer the chicken to the stockpot and bring to a boil. Add the fish balls, shallots, mushrooms, and lilies. Lastly, add strips of the dry bean curd sheet, the glass noodles, and the quail eggs and turn off the heat. Let simmer a few minutes.

4. Serve the soup very hot and garnished with pepper and chopped coriander. Set out more of the chopped coriander, lime wedges, roasted dried red chilli powder, and fish sauce to add as preferred.

Rakhine Ah Pu Shar Pu
HOT RAKHINE NOODLES

You cannot know the meaning of "hot" until you have tasted some of the Rakhine dishes. The name Ah Pu Shar Pu means "hot throat, hot tongue" and it is no exaggeration. However, you may omit the chilli pastes given below. The rice noodles are the same as for Monhinga so Japanese somen noodles can be substituted.

INGREDIENTS

4 servings of thin, soft rice noodles
5 cups fish stock made from scratch
1 pound firm-fleshed fish (the Rakhine use conger eel)
1 root galanga, lightly crushed
1/2 teaspoon of the best shrimp paste
6 cloves garlic, peeled and crushed
2 tablespoons oil
1/4 teaspoon turmeric powder
8 dried red chillies, stems and seeds removed

2 tablespoons oil
8 green chillies
2 tablespoons boiling water
Tamarind paste
1/4 cup garlic or onion oil ("Useful Information")
Roasted chickpea powder (·ditto·)
Chopped coriander
Pepper
Fish sauce

DIRECTIONS

1. Poach the fish with the galanga, garlic, and shrimp paste, then skin the fish and remove bones. Continue boiling the bones with the galanga, garlic, and shrimp paste. Sieve out bones.

2. Gently squeeze the fish flakes in a piece of white cotton cloth to remove any remaining liquid. Heat 2 tablespoons oil with the turmeric powder and fry the fish, stirring, until very dry and crumbly.

3. Soak the dried red chillies in a little hot water until soft and pound smooth. Heat 2 tablespoons oil and cook the red chilli paste until oil sizzles.

4. Pound the green chillies after removing stems and steep in 2 tablespoons boiling water.

5. To serve, put a serving of noodles in a bowl and top with a generous amount of the fish crumbs, 1 teaspoon of garlic or onion oil, ½ teaspoon or more tamarind paste as preferred, chopped coriander, and about ½ teaspoon fish sauce. Serve the soup separately or in the noodles as preferred.

If the noodles are served dry, add about ½ teaspoon roasted chickpea powder to each serving. Set out dishes of the red and green chilli pastes for guests to serve themselves. Serve the soup after removing the galanga root and sprinkling with lots of pepper.

Shan Khauk Swei
SHAN STICKY RICE NOODLES

This Shan noodle dish is so popular that it would be a shame to leave it out. The noodles are made with Shan rice, which is sticky. In the chicken stew the Shan use a spice mix very similar to five-spice powder, which is available in Chinese groceries.

INGREDIENTS

4 servings of dry or fresh rice noodles, stickier than ordinary rice noodles
1 pound chicken, skinned and cut into ¾-inch cubes, or 1 pound lean pork, chopped roughly
1/4 teaspoon fish sauce
1/2 cup oil
1/8 teaspoon turmeric powder
2 onions, peeled and sliced
4 cloves garlic, peeled and chopped
1 teaspoon salty pickled soybeans, ground to a paste
6 ripe tomatoes, peeled and blended to a paste
1/2 teaspoon sweet paprika
1 1/2 teaspoons five-spice powder

GARNISH

4 tablespoons roasted peanuts, crushed (optional)
Garlic oil ("Useful Information")
Blanched tendrils of the pea vine or blanched leaves of baby mustard greens

SOUP

4 cups rich chicken broth
5 cloves garlic, peeled and crushed
Salt to taste
Pepper
4 tablespoons chopped green onions

RELISH

Pickled mustard greens. Korean kimchi will do as well.

DIRECTIONS

1. Knead the chicken pieces or chopped pork with the fish sauce and set aside for 5 minutes.

2. Heat the oil with the turmeric powder and fry the onion slices until crisp. Drain and set aside. Fry the garlic in the oil until golden, add the soybean paste, and sweet paprika and cook for a few seconds. Add the fried onion slices, chicken or pork, and the tomato paste with ½ cup water. Simmer until the chicken is tender and the gravy is watery but thick. Just before removing the pot from heat, sprinkle with the five-spice powder.

3. Serve the noodles topped with a generous amount of the chicken and gravy, sprinkled with 1 tablespoon of the crushed peanuts if preferred, 1 teaspoon garlic oil, and garnished with some blanched pea leaves or baby mustard greens.

4. Serve the soup hot, sprinkled with the chopped green onions and pepper.

Shwedaung Khaut Swei
NOODLES OF SHWEDAUNG TOWN

Shwedaung is a small town in central Myanmar, made famous by the noodle dish that originated there and a Buddha image wearing eyeglasses. Apparently someone with poor eyesight donated them and improved his condition. This dish is a cousin of the Ohn No Khaut Swei coconut noodles, but you may omit the coconut cream, which is served separately.

INGREDIENTS
4 servings of egg noodles
1 pound chicken, skinned and cut into ¾-inch cubes
1 teaspoon fish sauce
1/4 cup oil
3 onions, peeled and chopped
2 cloves garlic, peeled and chopped
1/8 teaspoon turmeric powder
1/2 teaspoon sweet paprika
3 tablespoons roasted chickpea powder ("Useful Information")
1/2 cup water
Salt

DRESSING
4 teaspoons onion oil ("Useful Information")
2 cups coconut cream, cooked until thick nearly like curds with 1 tablespoon oil

GARNISH
A handful of egg noodles, deep-fried until crisp and almost brown
Chopped green onions

SOUP
4 cups rich chicken broth made from scratch, which can be done one day ahead

DIRECTIONS

1. Knead the chicken pieces thoroughly with the fish sauce and a little salt and set aside for 10 minutes.

2. Heat the oil with the turmeric powder and sauté the chopped onions for 1 minute. Add the garlic and in 1/2 minute add the sweet paprika. Almost immediately add the chicken with salt to taste and the roasted chickpea powder dissolved in 1/2 cup of water. Simmer until chicken is tender and the gravy is thick. This step can be done one day ahead.

3. To serve, place a serving of egg noodles in a bowl, dribble 1 teaspoon of the onion oil, and top with a generous amount of the cooked chicken and 2 tablespoons of the coconut cream. You may set out the coconut cream separately so that guests may take it to their liking.

4. Garnish with the fried noodle crisps and the chopped green onions. Some people like to pour a ladleful of the soup on the noodles and some serve it separately.

Kyay Oh
COPPER POT

This is a local dish that the fourth- or fifth-generation Chinese came up with in the late 1960s. Pork can be substituted with chicken. We cannot find exactly the same dish outside of Myanmar yet.

INGREDIENTS

4 servings of flat rice noodles or rice vermicelli, freshly made or boiled and drained

6 cups rich broth made from pork bones with 8 stalks Chinese coriander. This can be done one day ahead.

14 ounces ground pork, formed into balls with 1/4 cup sticky rice powder and salt to taste

5 ounces fish paste, formed into balls with 1 tablespoon sticky rice powder and salt to taste

3 1/2 ounces each liver, heart, and stomach of pork, washed and cut into strips

1 bunch baby mustard greens, cut into strips

4 small eggs (optional)

Light soy sauce

Chives, some cut into 1-inch lengths and some chopped

Pepper to taste

SAUCE

1/3 cup vinegar
20 green chillies, finely chopped
Salt to taste

FOR NOODLES SERVED DRY

8 teaspoons garlic oil ("Useful Information")
8 teaspoons fried garlic (-ditto-)

NOODLES IN SOUP

1. Put 1 serving of broth in a small pot on high heat, perhaps a copper-bottomed pot to make it authentic, and bring to a boil. When it is boiling hard, add the pork balls, heart, liver, and stomach strips and cook until the pork is done. Add the fish balls and in 2 minutes add the noodles.

2. Transfer the contents of the pot to a deep bowl and top with the greens, the chives, and pepper. Break one raw egg into the noodle soup if preferred. Serve light soy sauce separately to add as needed. Set out the vinegar-and-green-chilli sauce.

NOODLES SERVED DRY

1. Put 1 serving of broth in a small pot on high heat, perhaps a copper-bottomed one to make it authentic, and bring to a boil. When it is boiling hard, add the pork balls, heart, liver, and stomach strips and cook a few minutes until the pork is done. Add the fish balls and cook 2 more minutes, then sieve out the solids. Blanch the greens in the boiling soup and drain.

2. Put the freshly made or boiled noodles in a deep bowl and mix thoroughly with ½ teaspoon light soy sauce and 2 teaspoons each of garlic oil and fried garlic. Top with the pork balls, innards, fish balls, and finally the blanched greens. Serve the soup separately, garnished with the chopped chives.

Hsi Chet Khaut Swei
DELICATE EGG NOODLES WITH GARLIC OIL

This is a very popular Chinese dish sold from wooden pushcarts all over the country. Surprisingly, Myanmar friends who have traveled abroad tell me that so far they have not found anything exactly like it, even in China. I'm sure it must exist elsewhere outside of Myanmar.

INGREDIENTS
4 servings of the thinnest flat and soft egg noodles you can find. The best ones are flat and narrow, almost translucent, and somewhat crinkly.
1 pound boned duck meat
3 cloves garlic, peeled and crushed
2 slices ginger, cut again into strips
Light soy sauce

DRESSING
Garlic oil ("Useful Information")
Fried garlic, crushed finely (·ditto·)
Light soy sauce
Chopped chives
Salt

RELISH
2 onions, peeled and sliced
3 tablespoons lime juice or vinegar
2 green chillies, finely chopped
A little sugar
Salt

SOUP
4 cups clear chicken or duck broth, made from scratch with 3 cloves garlic peeled and crushed. This can be done one day ahead.
Salt
Pepper
Chopped chives

DIRECTIONS

1. Cut the duck into large pieces and wipe dry. Knead thoroughly with a little light soy sauce. Put in a bowl with some of the crushed garlic and the strips of ginger and place the bowl in a steamer. Steam for 1 hour or until very tender. Drain well, cool, and chop the duck meat into very fine pieces. This can be done one day ahead. Discard the fat from the pan juices and put the juices into the soup.

2. To serve, place a serving of the thin egg noodles in a bowl and add 1 teaspoon light soy sauce, 1 teaspoon garlic oil, and a few grains of salt. Mix thoroughly with a pair of chopsticks. Top with a liberal amount of the chopped duck, 1 teaspoon crushed fried garlic, and a sprinkling of chopped chives. Serve with clear soup garnished with chopped chives. For the relish, mix the onion slices with other ingredients.

Desserts

Daily meals normally do not end with dessert, apart from a lump of palm sugar or some fruits. The usual "dessert," especially for formal meals, is more likely to be a dish of pickled tea leaf salad. Sweets are mostly eaten as snacks or at teatime. One time that dessert is always served, and many varieties of it, is at the Soon Kyway ceremony of offering breakfast or lunch to Buddhist monks; then, the food offered is so plentiful that dishes cover the entire table. The same goes for home-cooked meals for invited guests. The desserts that follow for both occasions are as pretty and as scrumptious as the hostess can manage in showing off her skills.

Shwe Yin Aye
GOLDEN HEART COOLER

The Myanmar New Year falls in mid-April after five days' riotous celebration of the Thingyan Festival when we douse each other with water. Desserts are made by community organizations to distribute to all passersby, and families send out packed boxes to friends and neighbors. One favorite Thingyan dessert is the Golden Heart Cooler, especially enjoyed in the summer heat. Mother made it every single year when I was growing up.

INGREDIENTS

2 packets plain gelatine (or agar-agar)
Sugar to taste
Red and yellow food coloring
A few drops rose essence
2 cups water
1/2 cup sago seeds
1/3 cup sugar

1 1/2 cups sugar boiled in ½ cup water for syrup
1 cup cooked sticky rice
4 cups coconut cream
2 slices white bread, cut into quarters
Crushed ice

DIRECTIONS

1. Make firm red and yellow gelatine by using half the required water, flavoring it with a few drops of rose essence and sugar to taste. Cut into strips, keeping the colors separate.

2. Boil 2 cups water and stir in sago seeds until the white centers disappear. Stir in sugar and allow to set in a pan. Color the sago if preferred with a few drops of food coloring.

3. Dissolve 1 1/2 cups of sugar in a little boiling water to make thick syrup.

TO SERVE, place in each serving bowl:
    2 bread quarters
    4 tablespoons sago
    3 tablespoons sticky rice
    A liberal amount of the gelatine strips
    1 cup coconut cream
    sugar syrup to taste
    Top with the crushed ice

Thar Kway Yine

BLACK STICKY RICE WITH COCONUT

This is a dessert from the southern coast of Myanmar. Black sticky rice has a chewier texture and a different aroma than the white variety.

Thar Kway Yine literally means "swooning"—maybe from the rich taste or the aroma of the exotically pungent durian. Durian is a fruit with a thick, spiky shell hiding golden, custardy flesh wrapped around smooth seeds. It is also available cooked to a thick paste and sold in tubes in Asian stores. Durian may be omitted if preferred or substituted with ripe mangoes.

INGREDIENTS

3 cups cooked black sticky rice, kept warm
4 cups coconut cream
1/4 teaspoon salt
1 1/2 cups sugar cooked into a thick syrup
  with 1/2 cup water

Fresh durian flesh or slices of cooked paste

DIRECTIONS

Cook down the coconut cream on low heat until it just begins to separate and stir in the salt.

TO SERVE, place a serving of the black sticky rice in a bowl, spoon on a generous amount of the coconut cream and sugar syrup to taste, and garnish liberally with pieces of durian.

Shwe Ji Hsa Nwin Ma Kin
SEMOLINA CAKE

The name Hsa Nwin Ma Kin literally means "unavoidable turmeric," but not a speck of turmeric powder is to be found in the recipe. Quick-cooking oats can be used instead of semolina.

INGREDIENTS

1/2 cup fine but not powdery semolina, aka
  Cream of Wheat

1/2 cup sugar

1 cup coconut cream

1 cup warm water

3 well-beaten eggs

1/4 teaspoon salt

2 tablespoons ghee, aka clarified butter

2 tablespoons raisins

1/2 tablespoon butter

1 teaspoon white poppy seeds

DIRECTIONS

1. Toast the semolina in a pan until reddish golden. Mix the semolina, sugar, coconut cream, warm water, salt and beaten eggs in a bowl. Let stand for 30 minutes.

2. Heat the ghee in a wok. Add the semolina mixture and cook, stirring constantly until the semolina is thick and leaves the sides of the pan. Stir in the raisins.

3. Transfer to a 6-inch diameter cake pan. Smooth the surface, brush with ½ tablespoon butter, sprinkle with the poppy seeds, and bake in low heat for about 15 minutes until firm and the top is golden.

Pu Tin Thagu
SAGO WITH COCONUT PUDDING

Sago seeds set like gelatine beads and when topped with grilled coconut pudding, make a fragrant dessert.

INGREDIENTS

5 cups water
1 cup sago seeds
Hot water (if needed)
1 1/4 cups sugar
1/4 teaspoon salt

3 eggs
2 tablespoons flour
1 cup coconut cream

DIRECTIONS

1. Boil the water and add the sago seeds with the salt. Cook for about 15 or 20 minutes until thick. Stir often at that point and continue boiling until the white centers have almost disappeared, adding hot water as needed. Stir in 1 cup sugar and cook a few minutes more until thick again. Pour into a 8 x 8 x 2-inch cake pan to set.

2. Whisk the eggs with 1/4 cup sugar and fold in the flour. Add the coconut cream and stir until smooth. Cook on top of a double boiler until thick. Pour on top of the set sago seeds and grill until the top turns golden brown in patches. Chill before cutting.

Kauk Nyin Kin
GRILLED STICKY RICE

This is a popular street snack eaten on chilly days.

INGREDIENTS

1 cup uncooked sticky rice
½ cup water
1 cup coconut cream
¾ cup sugar
½ teaspoon salt

Banana leaves
Butter or oil
Wooden toothpicks soaked in water
Fresh coconut flakes (optional)

DIRECTIONS

1. Wash and drain the sticky rice and cook with the coconut cream, water, sugar, and salt. See "Rice" section for details.

2. Dip squares of the banana leaves in hot water to soften. Dry the underside, which is not shiny, with a clean cloth and rub butter or oil over it, thinly or thickly as desired.

3. Place 4 tablespoons of the cooked sticky rice in the center and wrap neatly and tightly into squares. Pin with the toothpicks. Grill on a charcoal fire until the leaves are charred in places. Serve sprinkled with coconut flakes if preferred.

Nget Pyaw Thee Paung
BRAISED BANANAS IN COCONUT

This is a rich but easy-to-prepare dessert.

INGREDIENTS

4 tablespoons butter
8 ripe bananas, peeled and pricked all over
4 tablespoons sugar
1/2 cup evaporated milk
1 cup coconut cream

1/4 teaspoon salt
1 cinnamon stick
3 cloves

DIRECTIONS

Heat the butter in a nonstick pan and fry the bananas until golden. Add the rest of the ingredients, lower heat, and simmer without stirring until almost all the liquid is absorbed. Remove the cinnamon and cloves. Serve warm or chilled as desired.

Mont Let Kauk Kyaw
GOLDEN BRACELETS

These are what you might call Myanmar doughnuts. Easy to make, they taste as good with honey as they do with jaggery syrup. Add 1 tablespoon rice powder to the dough if you want the bracelets to stay crisp longer.

INGREDIENTS

2 cups sticky rice powder (do not shake down)
1 cup water
1/4 teaspoon baking soda, aka soda bicarbonate
1/4 teaspoon salt

Oil for deep-frying
1 1/2 cups jaggery syrup ("Useful Information")

DIRECTIONS

1. Mix the sticky rice powder, water, baking soda, and salt into a dough and knead well. Divide into 16 balls.

2. Fill a wide wok more than halfway up with oil. Heat until the oil is hot, then remove pan from heat and let rest 3 minutes until the oil is cooler.

3. Roll each ball of dough into a 4-inch string, then coil and lightly touch the ends. Lay the coil gently in the oil. Continue until there are enough dough coils in the oil, but do not crowd them. Replace pan on heat. As the bracelets puff up, turn over and continue frying until deep golden on both sides. Lift out the bracelets with a chopstick through the hole.

4. Remove pan from heat and allow the oil to cool again for 3 minutes before making the next batch.

5. Serve immediately with jaggery syrup.

Mandalay Nget Pyaw Kyaw
MANDALAY-STYLE FRIED BANANAS

This too is easy to make and excellent served with black coffee. Yangon-style bananas are fried in a crisp batter.

INGREDIENTS

8 very ripe and soft bananas or plantains
1/4 cup butter
1/4 cup oil
2 cups coconut cream
1 teaspoon oil

4 tablespoons brown sugar
1/4 teaspoon salt

DIRECTIONS

1. Heat the butter and ¼ cup oil together in a nonstick flat pan. Add the peeled bananas but do not crowd. Do not turn them until well browned on one side. Turn gently and fry until golden dark brown on all sides. Drain.

2. Heat 1 teaspoon of oil in a separate pan and cook down the coconut cream until thick. Stir in the salt and brown sugar. Serve the fried bananas topped with the coconut cream. If preferred, omit the coconut cream and serve the bananas sprinkled with the sugar.

Thagu Lone
SAGO BALLS

Simple but pretty, they look like miniature snowballs if you leave them uncolored.

INGREDIENTS

5 cups water
1 cup sago seeds
Hot water (if needed)
1 cup sugar

1/4 teaspoon salt
2 cups grated coconut
A few drops vanilla or rose essence
Food coloring (optional)

DIRECTIONS

Boil the water and add the sago seeds with the salt. Cook, stirring constantly for about 15 or 20 minutes until thick and the white centers disappear, adding hot water as needed. Stir in the sugar, salt and essence and cook a few minutes more if it turns too watery. Pour into a pan to set. When cool, take up a lump with a teaspoon and roll in the grated coconut. You may add food coloring to the sago while still hot to make multicolored sweets.

Shwe Htamin Ngwe Htamin
GOLDEN RICE, SILVER RICE

The two served together make a teatime treat as delightful to look at as it is good to eat.

INGREDIENTS

1 cup uncooked sticky rice
1 1/2 cups water
1/2 cup white sugar
1/2 cup thick jaggery syrup ("Useful
   Information")

1 cup coconut flakes

DIRECTIONS

1. Cook the sticky rice with 1 1/2 cups water after washing well as directed in the "Rice" section. Let it cool a bit.

2. Take half the cooked sticky rice and knead well with sugar, and the other half with jaggery syrup. Press down hard into two buttered 4-inch pans and grill the tops until just golden.

3. Cut into diamonds and serve sprinkled with coconut.

Faluda
ROSE-SCENTED DESSERT

Although the name can be the same, I am not sure a dessert exactly like this Indian-style one exists outside of Myanmar. It is a beautiful, fragrant treat.

INGREDIENTS

1/2 cup milk
1 tablespoon flour
3 well-beaten eggs
3 tablespoons sugar
Vanilla beans or vanilla essence (desired
    amount)
5 cups milk, boiled down to 3 ½ cups,
    Keep chilled

4 big scoops of vanilla ice cream
1/2 cup strips of firm strawberry gelatine,
    using half the water required
2/3 cup boiled sago seeds, drained
1/2 cup crushed peanuts or cashew nuts
1 cup sweet rose syrup (available in Indian
    groceries)

DIRECTIONS

1. Cook 1/2 cup milk with the flour for 2 minutes until thick. Beat in eggs, sugar, and vanilla. Bake 20 minutes or until the top of the pudding is a dark golden brown.

2. To serve, in each tall glass put crushed nuts, 3 tablespoons of the sago seeds, 2 tablespoons of the gelatine strips, and 1/4 cup of the rose syrup. Pour on the chilled milk carefully and top with a chunk of pudding and a scoop of ice cream.

Snacks

Visitors to the country say that they see the Myanmar eating at all hours of the day. It is true that we do, but never appetizers just before a meal in the Western manner. Both Western-style cakes or pastries and the traditional rice cakes or crisps are readily available. We do not even need to go out to buy the snacks, as the rice cake sellers come right to our door or under our window. People living in high-rise apartments have a long string with a clip dangling down from their balconies so that the hawkers who come around even after midnight can tie the bag of goodies to the string to be hauled upward.

The dips that go with the snacks are given at the end of this chapter.

Pei Kyaw
CHICKPEA FITTERS

These are thin, round crisps studded with golden yellow chickpeas, delicious on their own or crumbled into a dish of Monhinga noodles.

SERVE with Tomato Sauce.

INGREDIENTS

1/3 cup chickpeas, soaked overnight and drained

BATTER

1/2 cup water
4 tablespoons rice flour
1/4 teaspoon salt
1/8 teaspoon turmeric powder
Oil for deep-frying

DIRECTIONS

1. Mix rice flour, water, turmeric powder, and salt and mix in the well-drained chickpeas.

2. Heat oil until hot and for each fritter, spoon in about 3 tablespoons of the chickpeas-and-batter mixture after stirring well. Do not crowd in the pan. Fry until golden, about 4 minutes, and drain on absorbent paper.

Boo Thee Kyaw
GOURD FRITTERS

The fresh taste of the gourd or chayote is enhanced by the light, crispy batter. It is one of the most popular fried snacks and is available all year round. It is also a favorite accompaniment for Monhinga noodles.

SERVE with Tamarind Sauce.

INGREDIENTS

1/4 of a gourd, peeled and cut into 1/2 x 1/2 x 3-inch lengths or 2 chayotes, peeled and cut into similar strips after discarding seeds and washing well

BATTER

Tempura powder made according to instructions and mixed with:
1 teaspoon chopped ginger
1 teaspoon rice powder
Oil for deep-frying

DIRECTIONS

Heat the oil and when hot, dip 4 or 5 pieces of gourd in the batter to coat completely and slide them carefully into the oil. Fry until golden on moderate heat, about 5 minutes. Drain on absorbent paper.

Yay Mont

WATER WAFER PANCAKES

Usually available only at pagoda festivals, the almost translucent and crisp Water Wafer Pancakes are a savory treat filled with peas and coriander. Use as flat a pan as possible and make sure to pour out any excess batter after it has coated the bottom in a thin layer. They are often served together with Gourd Fritters. No sauce is needed.

INGREDIENTS

1/2 cup rice flour (do not shake down)
1 1/2 tablespoons well-beaten egg
1/2 teaspoon salt
1 teaspoon finely chopped ginger
1 1/2 cups water

1 cup oil on hand
1 cup chopped coriander
1 cup chopped green onions
1 cup boiled garden peas

DIRECTIONS

1. Mix the rice flour, chopped ginger, salt, the well-beaten egg, and water until smooth. Stir well each time before pouring.

2. Heat a 7-inch nonstick pan and brush or spray the bottom with oil. When the pan is warm, pour about 3 tablespoons of the batter while swirling the pan so that the bottom is coated thinly. Replace pan on heat. As the pancake begins to cook, pour off excess batter if necessary. Sprinkle or spray the surface of the pancake with 1/2 teaspoon oil. If large holes appear, fix with a few drops of the batter.

3. When the edges turn crisp, lift up the sides carefully and dribble with 1/2 teaspoon oil so that it seeps under the pancake. Cook for about 4 minutes until crisp and light golden. Sprinkle half of the pancake with a little each of the chopped coriander, green onions, and peas. Fold pancake carefully in half, dribble a few drops of oil into the pan, and cook a few more seconds. Remove carefully. Before you make the next one allow the pan to cool a bit so it is no longer too hot, or you will not be able to make a thin enough Yay Mont.

Kyet Kyaw
FRIED CHICKEN

Fried chicken is an all-time favorite: as a side dish for a meal, eaten with steamed sticky rice, or as finger food with beer or toddy palm wine. The fish sauce works its magic to make this different from other finger-lickin' specialties.

SERVE with Red Chilli Sauce.

INGREDIENTS

2 pounds chicken, cut into small pieces
1/2 teaspoon turmeric powder
2 tablespoons fish sauce
1/4 teaspoon sugar
Salt

Oil for deep-frying

DIRECTIONS

Prick the chicken pieces with a fork and knead well with the turmeric powder, fish sauce, sugar, and very little salt. Marinate for 1 hour in the refrigerator. Heat oil in the deep fryer and when hot, fry the chicken pieces after shaking off the juices. Fry until red and crisp and drain on absorbent paper.

Pazun Gwet Kyaw

SHRIMPS ON GREEN NESTS

The red shrimps on dark green nests look as pretty as they are tasty. The leaves used in Myanmar are the Pazun Sar Ywet, "food for prawns," which literally grow by the roadside, but baby mustard greens without the stalks can be substituted.

SERVE warm with Tomato Sauce.

INGREDIENTS

12 shrimps, washed and dried
5 ounces baby mustard greens, cut into thin
 strips
Tempura batter made according to
 instructions

Oil for deep-frying

DIRECTIONS

1. Wash and dry the baby mustard greens. Peel the shrimps but leave the tails intact.

2. Heat the oil on a moderate flame. Dust the leaves with a little tempura flour, then add by spoonfuls to the batter and stir to coat thoroughly. Scoop up leaves and batter in a thin layer with a shallow spoon and carefully transfer into the hot oil.

3. Place a shrimp on this bed of greens after first dipping it in batter and frying until the shrimp is red and the edges of the fritter are crisp. Slosh some oil onto the surface of the fritter with a spatula from time to time. Drain on absorbent paper.

Ngar Galay Nga Yoke Thee Kyaw
ANCHOVIES WITH DRIED CHILLIES

Smelts or anchovies, both tiny fish, are available salted and sun-dried or fresh. Fried this way with chilli, they do not need a dipping sauce.

INGREDIENTS

6 dried red chillies, stems and seeds removed
3 1/2 ounces dried or 14 ounces fresh
   anchovies
Oil for deep-frying
1/4 teaspoon turmeric powder

3 cloves garlic, peeled and chopped roughly
1 teaspoon julienned ginger
Salt

DIRECTIONS

1. Soak the dried red chillies in hot water, drain, and pound or chop roughly.

2. Heat the oil with the turmeric powder and fry the dried anchovies for less than 1 minute. If using fresh ones, cut open the belly just under the neck and remove innards. Wash well and pat dry. Knead with salt and a little turmeric powder and deep-fry on moderate heat until crisp. Drain on absorbent paper.

3. Remove the pan from the heat and take out some oil so that about 2 tablespoons remain. Fry the garlic and ginger until fragrant and crisp, then add the chillies and fry a few seconds. Stir in the fish. Serve warm.

Tofu Hnat Pyan Kyaw
TWICE-FRIED TOFU

Traditional Myanmar tofu is made from chickpea powder, also known as channa dhal or gram powder, and not soybeans, although we have that variety as well. Without deep-frying, this tofu can be made into a salad (see "Salads" section).

SERVE with Lime or Vinegar Sauce.

INGREDIENTS

Tofu made according to directions in "Salads"
  section
Oil for deep-frying

DIRECTIONS

1. Cut the set tofu into ½-inch thick triangles, or squares about 2 x 2 x 3/4 inches. Slice them thinner if you want them crisper, but not so thin that they crumble.

2. Deep-fry the slices until golden, about 5 minutes. Drain on absorbent paper. Let cool and then deep fry again for 2 minutes or until golden red in color.

Pazun Nga Baung Kyaw
SHRIMP CAKES

Prawns and shrimps cook quickly and are perfect for easy-to-prepare snacks. This is one of the crisps sold by the Ah Kyaw Sone seller, together with gourd fritters, onion crisps, bean fritters, etc.

SERVE warm with Red Chilli Sauce.

INGREDIENTS

10 1/2 ounces small shrimps, unpeeled
Tempura batter made according to
   instructions
Oil for deep-frying

DIRECTIONS

1. Wash and drain the shrimps and trim off whiskers and legs. Pat dry.

2. Prepare the batter. In a serving spoon, mix 1 tablespoon of shrimp with 1 tablespoon of batter. Ease the shrimp-and-batter mix into the hot oil carefully so that the shrimp cake is flat.

3. Immediately prepare the next one and continue until the pan is full but not crowded. Fry for about 5 minutes until golden and crisp and drain on absorbent paper.

Kha Non Htoke
SHRIMP PARCELS

This was one of the favorite treats served for teatime or supper in the Royal Palace of Mandalay during the last Konebaung dynasty. The snack is believed to be of Thai origin.

SERVE with Lime or Vinegar Sauce.

INGREDIENTS

10 1/2 ounces shrimp meat, chopped
1 onion, peeled and chopped finely
4 cloves garlic, peeled and chopped finely
2 tablespoons oil
1/4 teaspoon salt

6 eggs
Salt
Pepper

DIRECTIONS

1. Heat the oil in a pan and sauté the onion and garlic for ½ minute. Add the chopped shrimps with salt and continue cooking until the shrimps turn pink and dry.

2. Beat the eggs with 1/4 teaspoon salt and pepper. Make a very thin crepe in a lightly oiled 8-inch nonstick pan. The pan should not be too hot so that the crepes will be thin.

3. In the center of each crepe place 2 tablespoons of the shrimp and fold into a parcel. Continue to cook on all sides until golden. Remove carefully and make the next crepe after oiling the pan.

M'Gyee Achin
TAMARIND SAUCE

You may use tamarind paste or powder and adjust the taste according to the product.

INGREDIENTS

4 tablespoons tamarind paste

1/3 cup warm water

4 cloves garlic, peeled and pounded

3 green chillies, pounded or sliced and stems
and seeds removed

1/2 teaspoon sugar

Salt

DIRECTIONS

Soak the tamarind paste in warm water. Mix the pounded garlic and chillies in the sieved tamarind paste with sugar and salt to taste.

Khayan Chin Thee Achin
TOMATO SAUCE

Grilling the tomatoes rather than boiling them imparts a delightful smoky flavor.

INGREDIENTS

4 ripe tomatoes

3 cloves garlic, peeled and pounded

2 green chillies, pounded and stems and seeds removed

2 tablespoons lime juice

1/2 teaspoon sugar

3 tablespoons chopped coriander

Salt

DIRECTIONS

Grill the tomatoes, remove the skin, and discard seeds if preferred. Whiz the tomatoes in the blender or chop finely. Mix the tomato paste with the pounded garlic and chilli, lime juice, sugar, and salt to taste. Stir in the chopped coriander.

Thanbaya Chin, Shalaka Yay Achin
LIME OR VINEGAR SAUCE

This sauce goes well with the Twice-Fried Tofu and Chinese-style noodles.

INGREDIENTS

5 cloves garlic, peeled and pounded
1 tablespoon pounded coriander leaves
4 green chillies, pounded and stems and seeds removed
Lime juice or vinegar to taste

1/2 teaspoon sugar
Salt

DIRECTIONS

Mix all the ingredients with salt to taste.

Nga Yoke Thee Achin
RED CHILLI SAUCE

This can be bought ready-made in bottles but can also be prepared at home, adjusting the flavor to taste. It goes well with Chinese-style noodles.

INGREDIENTS

8 dried red chillies, stems and seeds removed

5 cloves garlic, peeled and crushed

2 tablespoons sugar

2 tablespoons fish sauce

1/2 teaspoon salt

1/2 cup vinegar

DIRECTIONS

Boil the dried red chillies for 2 minutes in very little water until soft. Drain and whiz in the blender with the other ingredients until smooth.

Index

Defiled on the Ayeyarwaddy:
One Woman's Mid-Life Travel Adventures on Myanmar's Great River

As she approaches her sixties, Ma Thanegi decides to satisfy a lifelong dream. Jumping on any boat that would let her onboard, she begins a leisurely exploration of Myanmar's thirteen hundred-mile long Ayeyarwaddy River. Always hungry—for food, conversation, and a good story—Ma Thanegi clearly savors and vividly describes every adventure she encounters, whether she is traveling into the Cyclone Nargis-stricken delta region, feeding a dragon, or careening down the rock-infested white-water gorge of the Ayeyarwaddy's First Defile. You'll love accompanying this opinionated and delightful lady on an odyssey that takes her through much of Myanmar—never without great passion for her country, a wicked sense of humor, and her tube of red lipstick.

2010, ThingsAsian Press, 5 1/2 x 8 1/2 inches; 276 pages; paperback; color images
ISBN-10: 1-934159-24-7
ISBN-13: 978-1-934159-24-8
$12.95

Nor Iron Bars a Cage

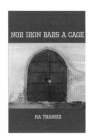

When Ma Thanegi was taken to Yangon's Insein Prison after working as a personal assistant to Daw Aung San Suu Kyi, she used every scrap of strength she possessed to adapt to incarceration without succumbing to despair.

The women prisoners who surrounded Ma Thanegi in Insein joined together, sharing food, support, and humor to get them through the ordeal they all faced. Buddhism helped them view their jailers with equanimity and the Myanmar values they had absorbed from birth allowed them to carry out a subtle form of protest—fashioning a nurturing community in a place that was designed to quell any sort of enjoyment.

From prostitutes to pickpockets to political prisoners, these women found ways to amuse each other, to be generous, to laugh within the walls of Insein. And chronicling this in her memory was Ma Thanegi, keeping her thoughts and observations in a mental notebook, waiting for the day when she could tell them to the world.

At last she is able to do that, with the honesty, insight, and irrepressible humor that permeates every book this talented woman has written. She describes the inner bravery and joie de vivre that served her and her fellow-prisoners well, in an account that provides a moving example of how to withstand times of crisis.

2013, ThingsAsian Press, 5 1/2 x 8 1/2 inches; 176 pages; paperback
ISBN-10: 1-934159-50-6
ISBN-13: 978-1-934159-50-7
$12.95

ThingsAsian Press

Experience Asia Through the Eyes of Travelers

"To know the road ahead, ask those coming back."
(CHINESE PROVERB)

East meets West at ThingsAsian Press, where the secrets of
Asia are revealed by the travelers who know them best. Writers
who have lived and worked in Asia. Writers with stories to tell
about basking on the beaches of Thailand, teaching English
conversation in the exclusive salons of Tokyo, trekking in
Bhutan, haggling with antique vendors in the back alleys of
Shanghai, eating spicy noodles on the streets of Jakarta,
photographing the children of Nepal, cycling the length of
Vietnam's Highway One, traveling through Laos on the mighty
Mekong, and falling in love on the island of Kyushu.

Inspired by the many expert, adventurous and independent
contributors who helped us build **ThingsAsian.com**, our
publications are intended for both active travelers and those
who journey vicariously, on the wings of words.

ThingsAsian Press specializes in travel stories, photo journals,
cultural anthologies, destination guides and children's books.
We are dedicated to assisting readers in exploring the cultures
of Asia through the eyes of experienced travelers.

www.thingsasianpress.com

To Vietnam With Love
A Travel Guide for the Connoisseur
Edited & with contributions by Kim Fay
Photographs by Julie Fay Ashborn

To Thailand With Love
A Travel Guide for the Connoisseur
Edited & with contributions by Nabanita Dutt
Photographs by Marc Schultz

To Cambodia With Love
A Travel Guide for the Connoisseur
Edited & with contributions by Andy Brouwer
Photographs by Tewfic El-Sawy

To Myanmar With Love
A Travel Guide for the Connoisseur
Edited & with contributions by Morgan Edwardson
Photographs by Steve Goodman

To North India With Love
A Travel Guide for the Connoisseur
Edited & with contributions by Nabanita Dutt
Photographs by Nana Chen

To Japan With Love
A Travel Guide for the Connoisseur
Edited & with contributions by Celeste Heiter
Photographs by Robert George

To Nepal With Love
A Travel Guide for the Connoisseur
Edited by Cristi Hegranes and Kim Fay
Photographs by Kraig Lieb

For more information, visit www.toasiawithlove.com